DEDUCT EVERYTHING!

DEDUCT EVERYTHING!

HUNDREDS OF TAX TIPS, LEGAL WRITE-OFFS, CREDITS, AND LOOPHOLES

TRACY BYRNES, MBA, CDFA

Humanix Books

Humanix Books

Deduct Everything! Hundreds of Tax Tips, Legal Write-Offs, Credits, and Loopholes
Copyright © 2026 by Humanix Books
All rights reserved

Humanix Books, P.O. Box 20989, West Palm Beach, FL 33416, USA
www.humanixbooks.com | info@humanixbooks.com

No part of this book may be reproduced or transmitted in any form or by any means, electronic or mechanical, including photocopying, recording, or by any other information storage and retrieval system, without written permission from the publisher.

Humanix Books is a division of Humanix Publishing, LLC. Its trademark, consisting of the word "Humanix," is registered in the Patent and Trademark Office and in other countries.

Disclaimer: The information presented in this book is meant to be used for general resource purposes only; it is not intended as specific financial advice for any individual and should not substitute for financial advice from a finance professional.

Portions of this book originally appeared in *Deduct Everything* by Eva Rosenberg (978-1-63006047-3), and *The Trump Tax Cut* by Eva Rosenberg (978-1-63006105-0).

Humanix Books titles may be purchased for educational, business, or sales promotional use. For information about special discounts for bulk purchases, please contact the Special Markets Department at info@humanixbooks.com.

Cover design: Ben Davis

ISBN: 978-163006-349-8 (Paperback)
ISBN: 978-163006-350-4 (E-book)

Printed in the United States of America
10 9 8 7 6 5 4 3 2 1

For David, Julia, and Celia,
Because even the most complicated things become manageable
when met with confidence, curiosity, and a sense of humor.
I love you most.

Contents

Author's Note xxxiii

Introduction xxxv

CHAPTER ONE
The Great Reset
Navigating the OBBBA Tax Landscape 1

TIP 1
Standard Deduction: Higher and Permanent (IRC 63(c)) . . . 2

TIP 2
SALT Deduction: A New Cap, a New Clock (IRC 164) 4

TIP 3
Personal Tax Rates: Still Lower, Still Favoring
High Earners (IRC 1) 4

TIP 4
Advisor Fees Aren't Deductible—And Charitable
Deductions Now Start After a "Floor". 5

TIP 5
Child Tax Credit: More Families Qualify,
More Refundable Cash (IRC 24) 5

TIP 6
Estate and Gift Tax: Stability Instead of Panic (IRC 2010(c); Treasury Regulation 20.2010-1(c)) 6

TIP 7
Business Owners: Cleaner Rules, Bigger QSBS Wins (IRC 199A and 1202). 8

TIP 8
Above-the-Line Deductions (2026–2028 Only) 10

TIP 9
The Mandatory Roth Catch-Up Rule: A Short-Term Hit for a Long-Term Win (IRC 219, 401) 11

TIP 10
IRS Digital Documentation Rules (IRC 6001, 6201) 12

CHAPTER TWO
From Cribs to Canes
How the OBBBA Unlocks Tax Breaks for Kids, Workers, and Retirees. **13**

TIP 11
Track Your Overtime Carefully—Only the Premium Is Deductible. 13

TIP 12
You May Deduct Up to $12,500 (Single) or $25,000 (Married Filing Jointly). 14

TIP 13
Your MAGI Affects Your Deduction 14

TIP 14
Keep Pay Stubs and Overtime Records Until Reporting Rules Are Final. 15

CONTENTS

TIP 15
Remember: You Still Owe FICA Taxes on All Overtime 15

TIP 16
Prepare to Track *Only* the Overtime Premium (the "Half") . . 15

TIP 17
Understand the Two-Year W-2 Reporting Transition 16

TIP 18
Do Not Reclassify Compensation: Beware of
Anti-Abuse Rules 17

TIP 19
Train HR and Payroll Teams Early 17

TIP 20
Understand That States May Not Follow Federal Rules 17

TIP 21
Supercharged Senior Deduction (the New $6,000 Bonus) . 18

TIP 22
More Social Security Benefits Stay Tax-Free
(the End of a 40-Year Problem) 19

TIP 23
Permanent 7.5% Medical Expense Threshold 20

TIP 24
The New RMD Standard 21

TIP 25
Bigger Catch-Up Contributions for Ages 60–68 22

TIP 26
Expanded Saver's Credit for Seniors Who "Un-Retire" 23

TIP 27
Expanded Qualified Charitable Distributions (QCDs)
(IRC § 408(d)(8)).................................25

TIP 28
Credits for Caregiving and Aging-in-Place
Financial Support................................26

TIP 29
Higher Deductions for Long-Term Care
Insurance Premiums..............................28

TIP 30
Maximize Annual Contributions ($5,000 Limit)........32

TIP 31
Look for a Potential Employer Match (Up to $2,500).....33

TIP 32
Prepare for Taxable Withdrawals After Age 18...........33

TIP 33
Expect Low-Cost, Index-Based Investments Only—
No Stock Picking, No Crypto.......................33

TIP 34
Don't Miss the Dell Foundation's $250 Seed Money
(for Older Kids) 34

CHAPTER THREE
Gratitude with a Garnish
How to Keep More of Your Tips Under the OBBBA 39

TIP 35
Keep a Daily Tip Record 40

CONTENTS

TIP 36
Report Cash Tips to Your Employer Monthly 40

TIP 37
New: Claim the $25,000 Tip Deduction (2025–2028) 41

TIP 38
Tips Are Still Subject to FICA (Always Have Been) 43

TIP 39
For Tip Pools, Only Report Your Net Tips 43

TIP 40
Understand "Uncollected FICA" on Your W-2 44

TIP 41
Report *All* Tips on Your 1040 (Even Noncash) 44

TIP 42
Pay Self-Employment Tax on Unreported Tips 45

TIP 43
Verify Allocated Tips on Your W-2 45

TIP 44
Self-Employed Workers Can Claim the $25,000
Tip Deduction 46

TIP 45
Electronic Tips (Venmo, Zelle, CashApp) Are
Fully Taxable 46

TIP 46
IRS Tip Monitoring Is Increasing Under OBBBA 47

TIP 47
Service Charges Are Not Tips 47

TIP 48
States May Not Follow the Federal Deduction 48

TIP 49
Keep Separate Logs if You Work Multiple Jobs 48

CHAPTER FOUR
The Family Fortune
20 Ways to Build a Tax-Smart Legacy for Your Inner Circle. . . 51

TIP 50
Child Tax Credit................................. 52

TIP 51
Child and Dependent Care (CDC) Credit 52

TIP 52
Earned Income Tax Credit (EITC) 52

TIP 53
Adoption Credit 53

TIP 54
The American Opportunity Tax Credit (AOTC)......... 53

TIP 55
The Lifetime Learning Credit (LLC)................. 53

TIP 56
Deduct Student Loan Interest....................... 54

TIP 57
Deduct Medical Expenses for Dependents 54

TIP 58
Deduct Charitable Driving Mileage 55

CONTENTS

TIP 59
Use That Dependent Care Account with Your Flexible Spending Account (FSA). 55

TIP 60
Beef Up Your Health Savings Account (HSA)—It's a Triple Tax Advantage Tool. 55

TIP 61
Take Advantage of the Newborn Savings Account (One Big Beautiful Bill Act Update) 56

TIP 62
Save for College (and *Way* More) with a 529 Plan. 56

TIP 63
Use 529 Funds for Student Loan Repayment 56

TIP 64
Put Your Kids on the Payroll. 57

TIP 65
Fund a Roth IRA for Your Child—The Ultimate Head Start. 57

TIP 66
Use the Annual Gift Tax Exclusion 57

TIP 67
Understand the "Kiddie Tax" Rule 58

TIP 68
File as Head of Household (HOH) if You Qualify 58

TIP 69
Check for Qualifying Widow(er) Status 58

CHAPTER FIVE
The Shelter Strategy
Maximizing Your Home as a Tax Shield Under the OBBBA . . 61

TIP 70
Exploit the Expanded SALT Deduction (OBBBA Update)   62

TIP 71
Deduct Mortgage Interest 62

TIP 72
Don't Forget to Use the $1 Million Limit on
Grandfathered Loans. 62

TIP 73
Use HELOC Interest for Home Improvement Only 63

TIP 74
Deduct Property Taxes Paid. 63

TIP 75
Deduct Private Mortgage Insurance (PMI) Premiums Again
(Starting 2026) 63

TIP 76
Deduct Mortgage Points on Purchase 64

TIP 77
Deduct Property Taxes Paid at Closing 64

TIP 78
Amortize Refinance Points over the Loan Life 64

TIP 79
Fully Deduct Prior Refi Points on Sale/Payoff 65

TIP 80
Add Most Closing Costs to Your Home's Basis 65

TIP 81
Deduct Interest Paid Before Closing 65

TIP 82
Deduct EV Charger Installation Costs
(Alternative Fuel Refueling Property Credit) 65

TIP 83
Maximize the Home Sale Exclusion to Minimize
Your Capital Gains at Sale 66

TIP 84
Claim a Partial Home Sale Exclusion 67

TIP 85
Keep Receipts to Increase Your Home's "Basis" 67

TIP 86
Deduct Medically Necessary Home Improvements
(Itemized Deduction) 68

TIP 87
Convert a Rental to a Primary Residence (for Exclusion) . . 68

CHAPTER SIX
The Rental Playbook
*Tax Hacks to Turn Your Property into
a Wealth-Building Machine* 71

TIP 88
Use the 14-Day Rental Loophole (IRC § 280A) 72

TIP 89
Deduct All "Ordinary and Necessary" Expenses
(IRC § 162) 72

TIP 90
Use Schedule C for Active Airbnb Hosting (IRC § 1402) . . 73

TIP 91
Use Schedule E for Long-Term Rentals (IRC § 469) 73

TIP 92
Separate Taxes for Business Use (IRC § 164) 74

TIP 93
Build Wealth Using Depreciation: The "Phantom
Deduction" (IRC § 167) 74

TIP 94
Deduct Costs of Attracting Guests (IRC § 162) 75

TIP 95
Deduct Travel Expenses for Rental Business (IRC § 162) . . 75

TIP 96
Move Personal Home Deductions to Your Rental
(IRC § 280A) 76

TIP 97
Account for Escrow Taxes on HUD-1 (IRC § 164) 77

TIP 98
Issue Form 1099-MISC for Service Providers
(IRC § 6041) 77

TIP 99
But—You Can Avoid Issuing 1099-MISC with Credit
Card Payments (IRC § 6050W) 78

CONTENTS   xvii

TIP 100
Deduct Interest on Time-Shares (IRC § 163) 79

TIP 101
Depreciate Qualified Improvements (IRC § 168) 79

TIP 102
Deduct Interest to Private Lenders (IRC § 6050H) 80

TIP 103
Prove Your Profit Motive (IRC § 183) 80

TIP 104
Understand Local Hotel/Lodging Taxes (State/Local Law) .. 81

TIP 105
Deposit Refinance Funds into a Business Account
(IRC § 163) 81

TIP 106
Report Unpaid Interest from Loans (IRC § 446) 82

TIP 107
Understand Passive Activity Loss Limitations (IRC § 469) .. 82

CHAPTER SEVEN
The Strategic Giver
How to Donate Like a Philanthropist and Save Like a Pro ... 85

TIP 108
Itemize to Deduct (Still the Gatekeeper) 85

TIP 109
Use the "Bunching" Strategy 86

TIP 110
Verify the Charity's Status 86

TIP 111
Keep Proper Documentation 86

TIP 112
Cash Donations: The Simplest and Cleanest
Charitable Deduction 87

TIP 113
Clothing and Household Goods: Condition and
Valuation Matter 88

TIP 114
Vehicle Donations: Special Rules, Lower Expectations 89

TIP 115
Deduct Only the Net Gift 90

TIP 116
Don't Donate "Losers" 90

TIP 117
Donate "Winners" (Appreciated Stock) 90

TIP 118
Understand the AGI Deduction Limits 91

TIP 119
Carry Forward Excess Gifts 91

TIP 120
Use a Qualified Charitable Distribution (QCD) 91

TIP 121
The Power of Donor-Advised Funds (DAFs) 92

TIP 122
Charitable Remainder Trusts (CRTs) 94

TIP 123
CRAT Vs. CRUT: Two Ways a CRT Can Pay You 95

CHAPTER EIGHT
The Hustle Shield
Self-Employed Tax Strategies to Protect Your Profits and Win Under the OBBBA 99

TIP 124
Deduct Business Meals at 50% 100

TIP 125
Separate Meal Costs from Entertainment 100

TIP 126
Deduct Meals for Transportation Workers at 80% 100

TIP 127
Deduct Business Mileage (Standard Rate) 101

TIP 128
Deduct Parking and Tolls Separately 102

TIP 129
Deduct Business Taxes Without a Cap 102

TIP 130
Deduct All Ordinary and Necessary Expenses 102

TIP 131
Deduct Business Travel Expenses. 103

TIP 132
Deduct Employee Safety Costs 103

TIP 133
Deduct a Portion of the Self-Employment Tax 103

TIP 134
Use the Optional Method for Social Security Credits 104

TIP 135
Claim the 20% Qualified Business Income
(QBI) Deduction 104

TIP 136
Understand the MAGI Limits for the QBI Deduction ... 105

TIP 137
Consider Becoming a C Corporation (C Corp) 105

TIP 138
Pay Yourself a Reasonable Salary (S Corporation Strategy) 106

TIP 139
Use the Cash Method of Accounting. 106

TIP 140
Maximize Section 179 Expensing 107

TIP 141
Include Used Property for Bonus Depreciation 107

TIP 142
Consider an Office-in-Home Deduction. 108

TIP 143
Take Advantage of the De Minimis Safe Harbor
(DMSH) Rule. 108

TIP 144
You Can't Have Access to an Employer Plan 110

TIP 145
Your Deduction Is Limited to Your Earned Income...... 110

CHAPTER NINE
The Investor's Edge
Mastering Capital Gains, Crypto, and the Stealth "NIIT" Tax 111

TIP 146
Try to Hold Investments Long Term.................. 112

TIP 147
Practice Tax-Loss Harvesting....................... 113

TIP 148
Manage Your Tax Bracket for Capital Gains 114

TIP 149
Donate Appreciated Assets to Charity................ 114

TIP 150
Follow the Wash Sale Rule (IRC §1091).............. 115

TIP 151
Use the Crypto Wash Sale Loophole—While It Lasts 116

TIP 152
Defer Tax on Mining and Staking 116

TIP 153
Take Advantage of the De Minimis Exemption—
If It Passes....................................... 117

TIP 154
Try to Hold Crypto for over a Year 117

CHAPTER TEN
Retirement and Wealth
Mandatory Roth and Long-Term Savings.................119

TIP 155
Maximize Contributions to Retirement Plans...........119

TIP 156
Contribute to a Roth IRA—If You Can 121

TIP 157
Take Advantage of the Backdoor Roth 122

TIP 158
Prioritize Roth Accounts for the Young'uns............122

TIP 159
Avoid IRA Early Withdrawal Penalties 123

TIP 160
Repay 401(k) Loans When You Leave a Job 123

TIP 161
Consider a Roth Conversion in Low-Income Years.......123

TIP 162
Use IRA Funds for Charitable Giving
(Qualified Charitable Distributions)..................124

TIP 163
Take Advantage of Higher Estate and Gift Tax Exclusions 124

TIP 164
Lower Your MAGI with Smart Contributions...........126

TIP 165
Use Roth Accounts Strategically 126

TIP 166
Use Tax-Loss Harvesting..........................127

TIP 167
Consider Municipal Bonds........................127

TIP 168
Don't Deduct Investment Fees or Tax Prep Costs.......129

TIP 169
Avoid Paying IRA Fees Out of Pocket................129

TIP 170
Same with Those Management Fees for Private Funds....130

TIP 171
Don't Miss Rollover Deadlines....................130

TIP 172
And Finally, a Roth Conversion Reminder............130

CHAPTER ELEVEN
The Triple Threat
Turning Your Health Savings Account into a Retirement Powerhouse............................131

TIP 173
The Power of the Triple Tax Advantage of Health Savings Accounts 131

CHAPTER TWELVE
The Fast Lane
Mastering the Road Rules for Maximum Auto Deductions..135

TIP 174
Start with Total Miles—No Fake Reverse-Odometer Tricks..136

TIP 175
Log Business Trips Like You're Planning the Perfect
Skip Day... 136

TIP 176
Standard Mileage Vs. Actual Expenses—You Get
to Choose... 136

TIP 177
Checklist to Pick a Method....................... 137

TIP 178
Luxury Car Depreciation Has Limits—Apologies to the
Ferrari Owners..................................... 138

TIP 179
Want a Big Deduction? Think SUV, Not Ferrari........ 139

TIP 180
A Home Office Turns Every Trip into a Business Trip.... 139

TIP 181
Rideshare Drivers Are Businesses—Even if It's a Side Gig.. 140

TIP 182
Yes, Even Cash Tips Count 140

TIP 183
Advertising Wrap? You've Turned Your Car into a Business
Asset... 141

TIP 184
Parking and Tolls—The Little Deductions That Add Up.. 141

TIP 185
Charitable Mileage—Doing Good Still Gets 14 Cents
per Mile 142

TIP 186
Charitable Parking and Tolls—Also Deductible 142

TIP 187
Medical Mileage. Sometimes Necessary,
Sometimes Deductible 143

TIP 188
Moving Expenses? Nope. 143

TIP 189
Standard Mileage Includes Depreciation—
Don't Forget This 143

TIP 190
Personal Property Taxes May Be Deductible—
If They Qualify 144

TIP 191
Buying Vs. Leasing? Run the Numbers 144

TIP 192
Employer Reimbursements Mean No Double Dipping... 144

CHAPTER THIRTEEN
Wait ... You Tried to Deduct What?
Debunking the Wildest Tax Myths in the Book 147

TIP 193
"My Dog Is My Security System—So He's a
Business Expense." 148

TIP 194
"I Can Deduct My Wedding Because I
Networked There." 148

TIP 195
"My Vacation Was a Business Trip Because I Talked About Work." 149

TIP 196
"I Bought Clothes for Work, So Therefore I Can Write Them Off." 149

TIP 197
"I Can Write Off My Kids Because They Help Me on TikTok." 149

TIP 198
"My Boat Is for Client Entertainment." 150

TIP 199
"I Can Deduct My Divorce Attorney. It's My Future Financial Planning!" 150

TIP 200
"I Can Write Off My House Because I Host Friends Who Talk About Business." 151

TIP 201
"My Gym Membership Is a Health Deduction." 151

TIP 202
"I Can Write Off My Dating App Subscriptions. They're Client Research." 152

TIP 203
"My Tattoo Is Advertising. It Has My Company Logo." .. 152

TIP 204
"My Pool Is a Medical Expense Because It Reduces My Stress." 152

TIP 205
"I Lost Money on Crypto, so I Don't Need to Report It." 153

TIP 206
"The IRS Doesn't Care About Side Cash." 153

TIP 207
"My Vacation Rental Losses Don't Matter Because It's Just a Hobby." 154

TIP 208
"I Don't Need Receipts. The IRS Trusts Me." 154

TIP 209
"If I Owe Less Than $1,000, They Won't Care." 154

TIP 210
"I Don't Have to File if I Didn't Make Much Money." . . . 155

TIP 211
"If I Get Audited, I'll Just Say My Accountant Did It." . . . 155

TIP 212
"The IRS Won't Notice. I'm Too Small." 156

CHAPTER FOURTEEN
The Great Extension
Mastering the April Deadline and Staying on Uncle Sam's Good Side 157

TIP 213
File Electronically. It's Faster, Safer, and Smarter 158

TIP 214
Uncle Sam Needs to Hear from You by April 15 158

TIP 215
Even if You Can't Pay Your Tax Bill—File Anyway! 159

TIP 216
Now, Even if You Extend, You Still Have to Pay
What You Owe 159

TIP 217
If You Owe, Make Your Payment Online 160

TIP 218
Set Up an IRS Payment Plan if You Can't Pay in Full 160

TIP 219
Short-Term Payment Extensions—The 180-Day
Grace Period 161

TIP 220
Paying with a Credit Card: Good Idea or Bad One? 161

TIP 221
Track Your Refund (or Payment) 162

TIP 222
All Refunds Aren't Instant—Even When You E-File 162

TIP 223
How to Fix a Mistake: Form 1040-X 162

TIP 224
Don't Forget to Amend Your State Return Too 163

TIP 225
The IRS Does Forgive Penalties—Sometimes 163

TIP 226
How IRS Interest Really Works—And Why the Penalty
Adds Up So Fast 163

TIP 227
Ignoring IRS Letters Doesn't Make Them Go Away 164

TIP 228
Create an IRS Online Account—It's Your Digital Tax Dashboard 164

TIP 229
Get an IRS Identity Protection PIN (IP PIN)—
Especially if You've Ever Been Hacked. 165

TIP 230
Know What "Injured Spouse" Means 166

TIP 231
Same with "Innocent Spouse" 167

TIP 232
And My Quick Public Service Announcement 168

TIP 233
Keep Your Tax Records—But Not Forever 169

TIP 234
Celebrate Responsibly—And Then Make a Note to Start Earlier Next Year. 169

CHAPTER FIFTEEN
The Goodfellas Guide to the IRS
Surviving an Audit Without Losing Your Cool 171

TIP 235
Reporting Round Numbers (aka "The $500 Rule"). 172

TIP 236
Large Deductions Compared with Your Income 172

TIP 237
Unreported 1099 Income 172

TIP 238
Claiming 100% Business Use of a Vehicle. 173

TIP 239
Excessive Meal and Entertainment Deductions 173

TIP 240
Home Office Abuse. 174

TIP 241
Cash-Heavy Businesses 174

TIP 242
Claiming the Earned Income Tax Credit
(EITC) Incorrectly 174

TIP 243
Amending Returns Every Year. 175

TIP 244
"Hobby" Businesses with Years of Losses 175

TIP 245
Don't Panic—An Audit Isn't an Indictment. 176

TIP 246
Know What Kind of Audit You're Dealing With 177

TIP 247
Respond Before the Deadline—Or Fuggedaboutit 177

TIP 248
Bring Receipts—Literally 177

TIP 249
Get a Professional—Your Consigliere 178

TIP 250
Don't Volunteer Extra Information 179

TIP 251
Get Everything in Writing—No Backroom Deals 179

TIP 252
You Can Appeal. Don't Let One Agent Be Judge
and Jury 179

TIP 253
Fix Whatever Triggered the Audit 180

TIP 254
Celebrate the Win—Even if You Owe Money 180

Conclusion.. 181

APPENDIX A
Recordkeeping That Actually Saves You Money 185

APPENDIX B
DIY Versus Hiring a Tax Pro......................... 189

APPENDIX C
I Need a Tax Pro 193

APPENDIX D
Think About State Taxes Before You Move 197

Acknowledgments 203
Index 205
About the Author 217

Author's Note

I hold an MBA in accounting, and before working directly with clients, I spent almost twenty years as a financial journalist covering taxes, markets, and economic policy. That experience gave me a front-row seat to how tax laws are written, debated, misunderstood, and—often—misused.

Today, I work with individuals, families, and business owners navigating real-life financial decisions through constantly changing rules, markets, and life transitions. I'm especially passionate about helping people feel confident about making those financial decisions—because understanding your money doesn't just change your balance sheet, it changes how you show up in your life.

This book reflects how I approach both journalism and financial planning: clear, practical, and grounded in real-world consequences—not theory, fear, or jargon—all with a little chuckle every now and then.

Deduct Everything! is educational and informational only. It is not personal tax advice.

Tax laws change frequently. IRS guidance evolves. State and local rules vary. And your individual financial situation matters.

Before acting on anything in this book, you should always consult your:

- CPA
- Tax preparer
- Financial advisor
- Another qualified tax professional who understands your full financial picture

For ongoing updates and commentary, visit tracybyrneswealth.com or the IRS website at irs.gov.

—Tracy Byrnes

Introduction

If taxes have ever made you feel overwhelmed, frustrated, or just plain confused—you're not alone.

The tax code isn't written for regular people. It's layered, technical, and constantly changing. And just when you think you've figured it out, Congress changes the rules again.

That's exactly what's happening now.

Starting in 2026, we enter a new tax era shaped by the One Big Beautiful Bill Act (OBBBA)—a sweeping overhaul that permanently resets many of the rules we've lived with since the Tax Cuts and Jobs Act.

Some changes are incredibly helpful. Others are completely nuanced. And a few can quietly cost you real money if you don't know they exist.

This book was written to help you make sense of all of it—calmly, clearly, and without panic.

And here's the thing: You do not need to become a tax expert to get through this. You just need to understand what matters, what's changed, and where smart planning can make a meaningful difference in your life.

So we will walk through the most important tax changes under OBBBA and how they show up in real life—not just in theory. Things like tax on tips, the Trump Accounts, and the new higher standard deduction. And we'll also cover the evergreen stuff—like how to extend your tax return, how to pay your tax bill if you're short on cash and what really happens if you're audited.

Big note: You don't need to read this book straight through or memorize it. Think of it as a guide you can return to when your income changes, when you're starting or selling a business, when you're planning for retirement, or when a tax headline makes things sound scarier than they need to be.

So if a particular section feels complicated, that's okay. Tax rules are layered by design. Awareness—not perfection—is what leads to better decisions.

DEDUCT EVERYTHING!

CHAPTER ONE

The Great Reset

Navigating the OBBBA Tax Landscape

What to Expect from the One Big Beautiful Bill Act

2026 isn't just another year on the tax calendar—it's the start of a complete financial reset.

After nearly a decade under the Tax Cuts and Jobs Act (TCJA), dozens of provisions were set to expire all at once, threatening to overhaul the tax landscape overnight.

The One Big Beautiful Bill Act (OBBBA) stepped in as the great rewrite, blending familiar rules with new reforms, tightening loopholes, and creating fresh opportunities for families, business owners, and long-term planners.

This moment is especially powerful for women. As we take the lead in financial decision-making, control more wealth, and launch businesses at record rates, understanding these shifts isn't just smart—it's empowering.

But this chapter gives everyone the clarity and confidence to navigate the 2026 reset with purpose, helping you make intentional choices that strengthen your liquidity, support your longevity, and protect your legacy for years to come.

So consider this your One Big Beautiful Overview.

Don't worry about memorizing this—this table is here to help you spot what's changed and what's worth paying attention to, not to turn you into a tax expert.

Pre-TCJA → TCJA → OBBBA

Category	Pre-TCJA	TCJA (2018–2025)	OBBBA (2026+)
Standard Deduction	Much lower	Nearly doubled	Higher + permanent
SALT Cap	Uncapped	$10,000 cap	$40,000 cap (temporary)
Top Tax Rate	39.6%	37%	37%
Misc. Itemized Fees	Allowed	Eliminated	Permanently disallowed
Child Tax Credit	$1,000	$2,000	Expanded + refundable
Estate and Gift Tax Exemption	~$5.6 million	~$13.6 million	$15 million
QSBS/Business Breaks	$10 million exclusion	20% deduction	$15 million + earlier tiers

You don't need to understand every line here—the tips that follow are where this becomes practical.

TIP 1

Standard Deduction: Higher and Permanent (IRC 63(c))

This bigger deduction means fewer people need to save receipts for charity, medical expenses, or job costs, since the standard deduction is automatic.

Because the threshold is indexed to inflation, it rises every year and protects lower- and middle-income households from bracket creep.

The flip side: Many people will no longer itemize, which changes how they should plan charitable giving or medical expense timing.

Standard Deduction: 2025 Versus 2026 Under OBBBA

Filing Status	2025 (per OBBBA)	2026 (per OBBBA)
Single (or married filing separately)	$15,750	$16,100
Married filing jointly (or surviving spouse)	$31,500	$32,200
Head of household	$23,625	$24,150

In simple terms: The standard deduction ticks up modestly in 2026, roughly *$350* more for singles (and similarly small increases for other statuses)—reflecting typical inflation adjustments.

What This Means (Especially Under OBBBA)

The higher standard-deduction baseline becomes permanent under OBBBA, meaning fewer people will need to itemize.

Because of this, many families who used to itemize (charity, mortgage interest, SALT, etc.) may see less benefit from itemizing, making planning around itemized deductions (like charitable giving or large medical expenses) more strategic than automatic.

Example: A single woman in New Jersey earning $80,000 previously itemized because her property taxes, charity donations, and medical bills exceeded the old standard deduction. Under OBBBA, in 2026 she'll simply take the higher standard deduction of $16,100 (because it is higher than her taxes, charitable giving, medical bills, etc.) and avoid the hassle and recordkeeping.

TIP 2

SALT Deduction: A New Cap, a New Clock (IRC 164)

The temporary $40,000 cap (2026–2029) helps homeowners in high-tax states regain deductions they lost under the $10,000 TCJA cap. But the phaseout at $500,000 MAGI (modified adjusted gross income) limits the benefit for high earners, making this a middle-class/upper-middle-class win more than a wealthy-family win.

And because the cap reverts to $10,000 in 2030, there is a built-in *expiration risk*.

Example: A married couple in Westchester, NY, paying $28,000 in property taxes and $12,000 in state income tax can now deduct the full $40,000 in 2026. But if their income rises above $500,000, they'll lose part of the benefit, making income/timing planning critical.

TIP 3

Personal Tax Rates: Still Lower, Still Favoring High Earners (IRC 1)

OBBBA keeps the TCJA's lower tax-rate structure, preventing rate spikes for most Americans. However, bracket thresholds move in ways that could push some taxpayers, especially dual-income professionals, into higher effective tax-rate territory.

The 37% bracket staying intact is a major benefit for high earners, but the middle brackets narrow slightly due to inflation indexing mechanics.

Example: A married couple earning $310,000 in combined wages may find themselves in a higher bracket quicker than in 2025 because the thresholds didn't rise as fast as wages. Meanwhile, a couple earning $700,000 is unaffected because the 37% bracket remains.

TIP 4

Advisor Fees Aren't Deductible—And Charitable Deductions Now Start After a "Floor"

Beginning in 2026, individuals cannot deduct investment advisory fees or tax preparation fees on their personal return. These costs are classified as miscellaneous itemized deductions and remain permanently disallowed under IRC §67(g).

At the same time, the OBBBA imposes two additional limits that affect higher-income itemizers.

- **Itemized deduction value is capped.** Taxpayers in the 37% bracket receive tax savings no greater than a 35% rate, even if their marginal rate is higher.
- **Charitable deductions are subject to a floor.** Itemizers may deduct charitable gifts only to the extent total contributions exceed 0.5% of adjusted gross income, under IRC §170(b)(1)(L).

Example: With $450,000 of AGI, the first $2,250 of charitable giving produces no deduction; is nondeductible.

TIP 5

Child Tax Credit: More Families Qualify, More Refundable Cash (IRC 24)

The boosted child tax credit (CTC) means more help for low- and moderate-income families, especially single parents. Inflation indexing ensures the credit doesn't lose value over time, a major flaw in previous versions. More families with young kids will get a refund even if they have low tax liability, ideally helping reduce child poverty rates.

Example: A single mother earning $52,000 with two children sees her refundable credit rise meaningfully, allowing her to use part of the refund to cover childcare or reduce credit card debt.

TIP 6

Estate and Gift Tax: Stability Instead of Panic
(IRC §2010(c); Treas. Reg. §20.2010-1(c))

The OBBBA's estate and gift tax exemption beginning in 2026—$15 million per person or $30 million per married couple, indexed for inflation—is welcome news. It prevents the federal exemption from dropping back down to roughly half of prior levels under the scheduled TCJA sunset and brings long-needed stability to estate planning.

This stabilized exemption keeps most families out of federal estate tax territory and significantly reduces the fear of an abrupt tax shock that had concerned planners and high-net-worth families for years.

The Nuance Wealthy Families Still Need to Understand

Although the exemption is now stabilized at a very high level, it is important to understand how it compares to prior rules—and how earlier planning decisions continue to affect estates today.

In 2025, before the OBBBA took effect, the federal exemption was historically elevated under TCJA-era rules and inflation adjustments. At that time, the exemption was approximately:

- $13.99 million per person
- $27.98 million per couple
  (IRC §2010(c), inflation-adjusted)

While 2025 has now passed, understanding that higher exemption remains essential. Many families made large lifetime gifts during that period, and the treatment of those gifts under current law is a critical planning consideration in 2026 and beyond.

The "No Clawback" Rule (A Major Planning Advantage)

Here's the key technical protection that continues to matter: the IRS has confirmed there is no clawback if you used a higher exemption amount when it was available and the exemption later changed.

Treas. Reg. §20.2010-1(c) provides that gifts made using a higher exemption are not retroactively pulled back into a taxable estate simply because exemption levels decrease in later years.

In plain English: If you used exemption when it was available, the IRS does not take it back.

Why This Matters

Lifetime gifting does more than remove the transferred asset from your estate. It also removes all future appreciation on that asset, which is often the most powerful estate-tax benefit. Over time, growth frequently dwarfs the value of the original gift.

Quick Comparison

- **2025 exemption.** Approximately $27.98 million per couple (TCJA-era, indexed)
- **2026 exemption (OBBBA).** $30 million per couple (OBBBA stabilized exemption)

Although the exemption remains very high today, understanding how prior planning fits into the current framework allows families to assess whether additional gifting, restructuring, or valuation strategies still make sense.

Example: A $32 Million Married Couple

Assume a married couple has a net worth of $32 million.

If no lifetime gifts were made and the available exemption is $30 million, $2 million may be subject to federal estate tax at rates up to 40%.

If the couple gifted $5 million in 2025 using the higher exemption available at the time, their remaining estate would be $27 million. Under today's $30 million exemption, the estate is fully sheltered, and the gifted assets—plus all future appreciation remain outside the estate permanently. No clawback applies.

Key Takeaways

- OBBBA provides exemption stability beginning in 2026.
- Prior gifting decisions remain legally protected.
- No clawback ensures earlier gifts stay outside the estate.
- The largest savings often come from removing future appreciation early.

This strategy is particularly effective for family businesses, real estate, pre-liquidity shares, fast-appreciating investments, and assets eligible for valuation discounts such as FLPs or LLCs.

TIP 7

Business Owners: Cleaner Rules, Bigger QSBS Wins
(IRC 199A and 1202)

Let's tackle the qualified business income deduction (QBID—pronounced "Q-BID") first. This next part is more advanced—not everyone will use this, but it's helpful to know it exists.

This was created under the TCJA to give small-business owners a tax break similar to what large corporations received.

It allows eligible business owners to deduct up to 20% of their business income on their tax return.

Who gets it? Owners of pass-through businesses such as:

- S corporations
- Partnerships
- Sole proprietorships (Schedule C)
- Some LLCs

What OBBBA changes:

- **Stricter definitions** for "specified service businesses" (like consultants, financial advisors, lawyers, doctors).
- **Tighter payroll/W-2 requirements**—you can't claim the deduction without paying yourself and employees properly.
- **Fewer loopholes** for high-income taxpayers who used complex structures to squeeze into the deduction.

So QBID still exists, but you need to have real payroll, a real business structure, and real documentation.

Now on to the qualified small business stock (QSBS) rules. These allow founders and early investors to exclude part—or *all*—of their gain from federal taxes when they sell shares of a qualifying start-up.

Seriously, this might be one of the best tax deals in the entire Internal Revenue Code.

Who qualifies?

- Founders of start-ups
- Early-stage investors
- Employees paid partly in stock
- Investors in companies with assets under $50 million at issuance

Now here is the *big* OBBBA upgrade: The OBBBA increases the exclusion to $15 million per issuer and adds new exclusion tiers:

- 50% exclusion after three years
- 75% exclusion after four years
- 100% exclusion after five years

It also allows stacking across multiple companies (each counted separately).

So if you build or invest in a qualifying small business and hold the stock long enough, you can sell part—or all—of it totally tax-free up to the new limits.

Example: A founder starts a company in 2021 and sells it in 2027 (a six-year holding period) for $12 million. The company's stock qualifies as QSBS under IRC 1202. Since the founder held the shares for more than five years, she qualifies for the 100% exclusion in OBBBA.

That means she pays *zero federal tax* on the entire $12 million gain. *What?!?!?!* Yep!!

This is why QSBS is one of the most powerful wealth-building tools for entrepreneurs (especially women founders who are launching businesses at record rates. Just saying.)

TIP 8

Above-the-Line Deductions (2026–2028 Only)

These temporary deductions help middle-class workers more than high earners because they reduce adjusted gross income, which drives Medicare premiums, credits, and phaseouts. So what are they?

- The tip-income deduction helps service workers directly.
- The overtime deduction helps those working long hours due to staffing shortages.
- The car-loan interest deduction provides breathing room for new buyers.

- Seniors get a meaningful boost with a new above-the-line deduction designed to offset inflation.

Example: A bartender earning $68,000 can deduct $8,000 in tip income above the line—instantly lowering AGI and preserving eligibility for premium tax credits.

See Chapter Three for more grist.

TIP 9

The Mandatory Roth Catch-Up Rule:
A Short-Term Hit for a Long-Term Win (IRC 219, 401)

The combination of higher contribution limits and the mandatory Roth catch-up rule for high earners is one of the most powerful and immediate shifts in retirement planning.

As a reminder, the 401(k)/Roth 401(k) contribution limits for 2026 are 24,500 plus the $8,000 catch-up = $32,500 if you are 50 or older.

If you are age 50 or older, and your Social Security (FICA) wages exceeded $150,000 in the prior calendar year (2025 wages), you are subject to the following mandate: The special age 50+ catch-up contribution (e.g., $8,000 in 2026) must be designated to a Roth.

What? Yep.

This rule forces a significant tax decision:

- **The short-term hit.** Making the catch-up contribution as Roth means you cannot take an immediate tax deduction. You must pay federal and state income tax on that $8,000 in the year you contribute it. This is why it feels like a short-term hit.
- **The long-term win.** This tax paid up front buys you a massive advantage—tax-free compounding for life. Because

the money is in a Roth account, all growth and subsequent withdrawals in retirement (after age 59½ and meeting the five-year rule) will be completely tax-free. For high earners expecting to be in a high tax bracket during retirement, this is an undeniable long-term victory.

But there is a *big heads-up for small businesses!* This rule creates a nonnegotiable compliance deadline for employers: To facilitate this rule, all retirement plans must offer a Roth contribution feature.

Small businesses that fail to update their plans to offer a Roth option by the end of 2026 will unintentionally cause all their high-earning employees (those over the $150,000 wage threshold) to lose the ability to make *any* catch-up contributions. This is a severe penalty for employees and a major compliance risk for the business.

Ugh.

Example: A 58-year-old earning $220,000 in 2025 must make her $8,000 catch-up contribution as a Roth in 2026. She pays income tax on that $8,000 now, but she has secured tax-free withdrawals on all future earnings for the rest of her life. If her small business fails to offer a Roth option, she loses the $8,000 catch-up contribution room entirely.

TIP 10

IRS Digital Documentation Rules (IRC 6001, 6201)

The IRS is modernizing its systems to match documentation in real time—meaning mileage logs, charitable receipts, and certain energy-credit records must be digital.

Paper shoeboxes won't cut it anymore (thankfully!). It's better for you anyway. Digitalization also reduces audit stress: If you have digital proof, matching happens automatically.

Example: A rideshare driver using a mileage app meets the new requirements perfectly, so no need to re-create logs or guess total miles.

CHAPTER TWO

From Cribs to Canes

How the OBBBA Unlocks Tax Breaks for Kids, Workers, and Retirees

Five Tax Tips for Employees Working Overtime Under the OBBBA

TIP 11

Track Your Overtime Carefully—
Only the Premium Is Deductible

The One Big Beautiful Bill Act deduction is limited to overtime that qualifies under the federal Fair Labor Standards Act (FLSA) rules, and that's actually a much narrower category than most people realize.

The FLSA sets the basic federal rule that most hourly workers must be paid time and a half for any hours worked over 40 in a workweek.

The new deduction applies only to the "half," the extra portion of your overtime pay—basically the amount paid more than your regular hourly rate.

If this feels complicated, that's because it is—and it's also why planning matters. As an example, let's say you are paid $20/hour. Your overtime, time and a half, brings you to $30/hour.

Only that $10 premium is deductible, *not* the full overtime wage.

Overtime triggered by state laws, union agreements, or employer policies may not qualify unless the IRS expands the definition. Because official guidance is still evolving, keep detailed pay stubs and ask HR which categories of overtime your company uses.

TIP 12

You May Deduct Up to $12,500 (Single) or $25,000 (Married Filing Jointly)

The OBBBA gives eligible hourly workers a rare opportunity to deduct a significant portion of their FLSA overtime premium from federal taxes. This deduction is "above the line," meaning you do not need to itemize to take advantage of it.

The maximum benefit is capped at $12,500 (as a single person) or $25,000 (as a couple married filing jointly).

However, the deduction only applies for 2025–2028, so it's a temporary tax break. Be intentional about maximizing it during these qualifying years.

TIP 13

Your MAGI Affects Your Deduction

The deduction is not available to high earners. Once your modified adjusted gross income passes $150,000 (single) or $300,000 (married filing jointly), the overtime deduction begins to phase out.

The allowable deduction is reduced by $100 for every $1,000 that your MAGI exceeds the threshold.

If you are near the limit, boosting retirement contributions or HSA contributions may lower your MAGI enough to maximize the deduction. Planning ahead can make a big difference in how much of the benefit you receive.

TIP 14

Keep Pay Stubs and Overtime Records Until Reporting Rules Are Final

Since the IRS has not yet clarified how "qualified overtime" must appear on your W-2 for the 2025 tax year, you should save your pay reports for each pay period.

Having your own record ensures you can verify what portion of your overtime premium is eligible for the deduction. This protects you in case of any misreporting or if the IRS guidance shifts after the year begins. Good recordkeeping now avoids tax-season headaches later.

TIP 15

Remember: You Still Owe FICA Taxes on All Overtime

The overtime deduction reduces your federal income tax, but it does not reduce Social Security or Medicare (FICA) withholding.

This means your paycheck will still show full FICA on every dollar of overtime you earn.

Five Tax Tips for Employers Under the OBBBA Overtime Deduction

TIP 16

Prepare to Track *Only* the Overtime Premium (the "Half")

Payroll systems must be ready to distinguish the federal FLSA overtime premium from all other categories of pay. As mentioned above, the deduction applies only to the premium portion (the "half" in "time and a half") of overtime required under the Fair Labor Standards Act.

Overtime generated by state daily rules, union agreements, or internal employer policies does not qualify.

Employers who fail to separate these categories—or who report the entire overtime wage instead of just the premium—will cause employee tax filing errors.

Start working with payroll vendors now to ensure they can calculate and separate the FLSA premium amount.

TIP 17

Understand the Two-Year W-2 Reporting Transition

The IRS requires that the qualified overtime deduction amount be accurately reported to employees, but the implementation is phased:

- **For tax year 2025 (transition year).** The IRS has issued penalty relief for failure to use a separate W-2 box. However, employers are *strongly encouraged* to provide a separate accounting of this figure to employees (e.g., in Box 14 or on a separate year-end statement) so employees can accurately claim the deduction.
- **For tax year 2026 and beyond.** Mandatory separate reporting is expected to be required on the updated W-2.

Companies should use this transition year to test internal tracking methods and coordinate with payroll vendors to ensure readiness for the mandatory 2026 reporting.

TIP 18

Do Not Reclassify Compensation: Beware of Anti-Abuse Rules

Employers must avoid the temptation to restructure pay to help employees out. Things like reclassification of regular wages, shift differentials, or bonuses as "FLSA overtime" to maximize employee deductions may cause red flags.

The IRS is expected to issue strong anti-abuse rules to penalize employers that intentionally manipulate pay structures.

The safest approach is to maintain existing compensation structures until all formal guidance is released. Communicate this compliance risk clearly to managers to protect the company from liability.

TIP 19

Train HR and Payroll Teams Early

Let's face it—employees are going to have a ton of questions about whether their specific overtime qualifies.

HR professionals need to understand the distinctions between federal, state, and employer-driven overtime rules. Payroll staff will need new processes for tracking, categorizing, and reporting eligible overtime.

Providing training early will prevent misinformation and make tax season smoother for everyone.

TIP 20

Understand That States May Not Follow Federal Rules

The OBBBA overtime deduction is a federal benefit, and states can choose not to adopt it.

This means employees may get a tax break at the federal level but still owe full state tax on overtime wages.

This will not make them happy, so be sure to avoid guaranteeing that overtime will be "tax-free" or "tax-reduced" without clarifying whether the specific state conforms.

The Grumpy Old Men Guide to Smarter Senior Taxes Under the OBBBA

If you've ever watched *Grumpy Old Men*, you know aging comes with creaky joints, sharp mouths, and surprising plot twists. Max and John spend their days fishing, arguing, and chasing Ariel as if they're still 25, proof that getting older doesn't mean slowing down.

It just means the rules change.

And nowhere do the rules get more confusing than the IRS.

Fortunately, the One Big Beautiful Bill Act delivers a set of new, senior-friendly tax rules that give older Americans more breathing room—more deductions, more flexibility, more credits, and fewer reasons to grumble.

TIP 21

Supercharged Senior Deduction (the New $6,000 Bonus)

The OBBBA gives taxpayers 65+ an additional $6,000 deduction on top of the already-increased standard deduction, creating a massive automatic write-off.

Baseline Rule (Under 65)

For 2025, the standard deduction for younger filers is set at:

- $15,750 (single)

- $31,500 (married filing jointly)
- $23,625 (head of household)

There also has been a long-standing, pre-OBBBA benefit for being 65 or older. For a single filer in 2025, this amount is $2,000. (This deduction is also granted if you are legally blind.)

Why OBBBA Helps Seniors

Most retirees no longer itemize because they've paid off mortgages and spend less on deductible expenses. The OBBBA makes the senior standard deduction so large that many can stop itemizing entirely. A qualifying single senior can potentially deduct up to $23,750 for 2025! (This includes the base $15,750, the original 65+ $2,000 age-based deduction, and the OBBBA's new $6,000 bonus.)

Example: Marie, 68, has only $8,000 of itemized deductions. Her new combined senior standard deduction of up to $23,750 eliminates the need to track receipts and ensures that she gets the maximum tax break available.

TIP 22

More Social Security Benefits Stay Tax-Free (the End of a 40-Year Problem)

The OBBBA finally modernizes the taxation thresholds for Social Security benefits by providing a large deduction that effectively ensures that far fewer seniors are taxed on this critical income source.

Baseline Rule (the Outdated Tax Trap)

Since 1983, Social Security taxation has been based on fixed thresholds that have never been indexed for inflation. This created the "Social Security tax trap": If your combined income (AGI + tax-exempt interest + half of your Social Security) exceeds $25,000 (single) or $32,000 (married filing jointly), up to 50% of your benefits can be taxed. Or if income exceeds a second, higher threshold ($34,000 single/$44,000 married), up to 85% of benefits can be taxed.

Why OBBBA Helps Seniors

The new deduction ensures that the total tax breaks available to seniors exceed the average retirement benefit received. This ensures that after years of hard work, seniors can keep more of their Social Security income.

The OBBBA provides a new, large deduction that pushes your total taxable income back below those fixed 1983 thresholds. This effectively neutralizes the outdated tax trap for the vast majority of retirees, meaning they can collect their benefits and still withdraw a reasonable amount from their IRA or 401(k) without suddenly making their Social Security taxable.

This relief means only about 12% of seniors will pay taxes on their benefits.

Example (averting the trap): Helen receives the average Social Security benefit (approximately $24,000) and files as a single taxpayer.

Under the outdated rules, even a small withdrawal from her IRA could push her over the $25,000 single threshold, making up to 50% of her Social Security benefits taxable.

Under the updated OBBBA-enhanced deductions, none of her benefits are taxable, giving her back the full value of her Social Security check.

TIP 23

Permanent 7.5% Medical Expense Threshold

The OBBBA permanently locks the medical deduction floor at 7.5% of adjusted gross income.

Baseline Rule

For years, the medical deduction threshold bounced between 7.5% and 10%, creating confusion. Without this permanent fix, the law was scheduled to revert to 10%, which would have prevented many seniors from claiming deductions entirely.

Why OBBBA Helps Seniors

By guaranteeing a permanent 7.5% floor, seniors with high out-of-pocket healthcare costs—a reality of aging—finally get predictable and meaningful relief. You only deduct costs that exceed this percentage of your AGI.

Example: Carlos earns $60,000 and has $7,000 in medical costs. With the 7.5% threshold, his floor is $4,500. He gets to deduct $2,500 ($7,000 - $4,500), savings he would have lost under the old 10% threshold.

TIP 24

The New RMD Standard

Required minimum distribution (RMD) rules have been evolving for years, and understanding the current framework matters for retirement planning.

Under SECURE Act 2.0, the RMD start age depends on your birth year.

- Individuals born between 1951 and 1959 must begin RMDs at age 73.
- Those born in 1960 or later will have an RMD age of 75, although that rule does not fully take effect until 2033.

This staggered schedule created confusion and uneven outcomes for retirees in different age cohorts.

Why this matters: Delaying RMDs provides meaningful planning advantages. Fewer forced withdrawals mean more time for tax-deferred accounts to grow, a longer window for strategic Roth conversions in lower tax brackets, and improved control over taxable income in retirement.

Example: Diane, born in 1953, must begin RMDs at 73 under current law. However, knowing future rules allows her to proactively plan conversions, manage brackets, and coordinate withdrawals more efficiently before mandatory distributions accelerate later.

TIP 25

Bigger Catch-Up Contributions for Ages 60–68

The OBBBA creates a supercharged catch-up window for late-stage savers who are working and need to make up for lost time.

Baseline Rule (Age 50+)

The typical age 50+ catch-up contribution is $8,000—that is projected, in addition to the also projected regular $24,500 401(k) limit for 2026. The total limit then is $32,500.

Why OBBBA Helps Seniors

Between ages 60 and 63, individuals are now eligible for an even higher catch-up cap of $11,250—meaning they can stash thousands more into pre-tax accounts. This supercharged window is ideal for those who "un-retire" or those needing a final boost before permanently stopping work.

Example: Robert, 62, returns to work part-time. OBBBA's expanded limits allow him to contribute $35,750, which is well above the normal $32,500 and lowers his current taxable income while aggressively boosting his nest egg.

TIP 26

Expanded Saver's Credit for Seniors Who "Un-Retire"

The OBBBA makes the Saver's Credit a significantly better deal for older workers who pick up part-time work and save. This credit is set to transform into the highly beneficial Saver's Match in 2027.

Baseline Rule (Through 2026)

The original Retirement Savings Contributions Credit (the Saver's Credit) equals 10%, 20%, or 50% of contributions (up to a maximum contribution of $2,000 per person).

This credit is nonrefundable, meaning you only receive a benefit if you owe tax, a limitation that has historically made it ineffective for low-income seniors.

Why OBBBA Helps Seniors

The OBBBA increases the modified adjusted gross income thresholds for the highest credit rates. This means more part-time working seniors qualify for the valuable rates.

The 50% rate is available for a couple filing jointly in 2025 with MAGI up to $47,500.

The Future (Starting 2027)—The Saver's Match: This credit will be replaced by the Saver's Match. The match is a government contribution of up to 50% of your savings (max $1,000) deposited directly into your retirement account. This is fully refundable, meaning eligible seniors will receive the full benefit as cash in their retirement accounts, even if their tax bill is zero.

Example: Linda, 67, works part-time and contributes $2,000 to an IRA. Assuming her income qualifies, under the OBBBA's current rules (2025/2026), she receives a tax credit worth up to $1,000. Starting in 2027, the Saver's Match will automatically deposit the matching cash directly into her IRA, aggressively encouraging saving and building real wealth at any age.

WHAT IS THE SAVER'S CREDIT? (IRS FORM 8880)

The Saver's Credit (Retirement Savings Contributions Credit) is essentially a government match designed to reward low- and moderate-income taxpayers for setting money aside for retirement. It's calculated on IRS Form 8880.

How the Credit Works

The credit is one of the most effective tax breaks because it is a tax credit, not a deduction.

Credit vs. deduction: As a reminder, unlike a deduction, which only reduces your taxable income, a credit reduces your actual tax bill dollar-for-dollar. That's way better.

The match: The credit is calculated as a percentage of your contributions up to $2,000 per person (or $4,000 if married filing jointly).

The percentage you receive is based on your adjusted gross income:

- 50% rate—highest benefit for the lowest income levels
- 20% rate
- 10% rate—lowest benefit for the highest income levels

The Current Problem with the Credit (Through 2026)

Currently, the credit is nonrefundable.

This is the most important caveat: A nonrefundable credit can only reduce the taxes you owe down to zero; it cannot generate a refund or add to one. This has historically meant that many low-income taxpayers, who owe little or no federal income tax anyway, could not fully benefit from the credit.

The Future Game-Changer (the Saver's Match, 2027)
The OBBBA-related changes are currently boosting the eligibility of the *existing* credit (as explained earlier in Tip 26), but the ultimate change comes in 2027. That's when the credit will be replaced by the Saver's Match, which is a *fully refundable cash contribution.*

Instead of reducing your tax bill, the government will deposit the matching funds directly into your retirement account (up to $1,000 per person). This removes the nonrefundable barrier, giving eligible workers a real cash match regardless of their tax liability.

TIP 27

Expanded Qualified Charitable Distributions (QCDs) (IRC §408(d)(8))

The OBBBA reinforces the Qualified Charitable Distribution (QCD) as one of the most tax-efficient ways for seniors to give—especially as new limits reduce the value of traditional itemized charitable deductions for higher-income taxpayers.

Baseline Rule

QCDs are available starting at age 70½ and must be made directly from an IRA to a qualified charity. The annual QCD limit is over $100,000 per person and is permanently indexed for inflation, allowing larger tax-free charitable transfers over time.

The Strategic Rationale (Why It Makes Sense)

If you are charitable and do not need income from your tax-deferred IRA, a QCD is powerful for two primary reasons.

First, it can satisfy all or part of your required minimum distribution without increasing taxable income. When RMDs apply, the QCD counts toward the required withdrawal, but the distribution itself is excluded from taxable income.

Second, it keeps adjusted gross income lower. Because QCDs never enter AGI, they can quietly generate additional tax savings that often go unnoticed, including:

- Reducing the taxable portion of Social Security benefits
- Lowering Medicare premium surcharges (IRMAA)
- Avoiding the impact of new itemized deduction limits, since a QCD is not an itemized deduction

Example: Frank, age 75, directs $15,000 from his IRA straight to a qualified charity. The transfer never appears in his AGI, often producing a better overall tax result than writing a personal check and attempting to claim a deduction later.

OBBBA's New Legacy Option

The OBBBA also introduces a one-time QCD opportunity of up to $54,000 that may be used to fund certain split-interest charitable gifts, such as a charitable remainder trust or charitable gift annuity, allowing retirees to combine tax efficiency with long-term legacy planning.

TIP 28

Credits for Caregiving and Aging-in-Place Financial Support

The One Big Beautiful Bill Act strengthens tax support for families managing eldercare and for seniors who want to remain safely in their homes longer.

It does this primarily through an expanded *caregiving tax credit*, paired with broader *age-based tax relief for medical expenses* (also discussed earlier in this book):

Expanded Credit for Care Services (Child and Dependent Care Tax Credit)

The Child and Dependent Care Tax Credit (CDCTC) helps working taxpayers offset the cost of professional care. The OBBBA significantly enhances this credit.

What's changing. Beginning in 2026, the maximum credit rate increases from 35% to 50% of eligible expenses for lower-income households.

Why this matters for eldercare. This credit applies not only to childcare, but also when you pay for care for an elderly dependent, such as a parent, so that you or your spouse can work.

Credit value:

- Up to $3,000 of expenses for one dependent
- Up to $6,000 for two or more dependents

And remember, because this is a tax credit, it reduces your tax bill dollar-for-dollar, making it one of the most powerful tools available to working caregivers.

Aging-in-Place Reality Check: Why Cash-Flow Relief Matters More Than Medical Deductions

Many aging-in-place expenses, such as stair lifts, grab bars, or home safety upgrades, are technically medical expenses, but they are often not deductible in practice.

Medical deductions generally only apply once costs exceed 7.5% of adjusted gross income, a threshold many retirees never reach.

As discussed earlier, age-based deductions under the OBBBA can improve overall retirement cash flow even though they are not tied to specific medical spending, helping seniors absorb these costs without relying on hard-to-use medical deductions.

Example of aging in place, simplified: Susan installs a stair lift and grab bars so she can remain safely in her home. Under traditional rules, these expenses would only provide tax relief if her total medical costs exceeded the 7.5% AGI threshold, something that often doesn't happen. Instead, broader senior tax relief improves Susan's overall tax picture, reducing the taxes she pays on Social Security and IRA withdrawals and freeing up cash flow to cover her home modifications without complex deduction calculations.

Why This Matters

Caregiving and aging in place rarely fit neatly into the tax code. The OBBBA improves the landscape by:

- Strengthening direct credits for working caregivers
- Improving overall tax flexibility for seniors, making it easier to fund safety, independence, and dignity at home

TIP 29

Higher Deductions for Long-Term Care Insurance Premiums

Long-term care is one of the largest and most unpredictable financial risks in retirement. As premiums rise and coverage becomes harder to replace later in life, the tax treatment of insurance matters more than ever.

The OBBBA improves this planning tool by allowing a greater portion of LTC premiums to count toward deductible medical expenses—bringing tax relief closer to the real cost of coverage.

Baseline Rule: LTC Premiums Are Deductible, but Only Up to Strict Age-Based Limits

Under current IRS rules, qualified long-term care insurance premiums are treated as medical expenses and may be included on Schedule A.

However, the amount that counts is:

- Capped annually based on age
- Only useful if total medical expenses exceed 7.5% of AGI.

For tax year 2025, the IRS allows the following maximum amounts *per person* to be counted as medical expenses:

Age at Year-End	2025 IRS Deductible Limit
61–70	$4,810
71+	$6,020

These limits increase with age, but for many seniors they still fall below actual premium costs, meaning a portion of LTC insurance spending often receives no tax benefit at all.

Enter the OBBBA

The OBBBA raises the age-based deductibility caps for long-term care insurance premiums, allowing seniors to count more of what they actually pay toward deductible medical expenses.

Rather than replacing the existing structure, the OBBBA wakes up to reality, acknowledging that:

- LTC premiums have risen significantly.
- The likelihood of needing care increases sharply later in life.

By increasing these caps, the OBBBA improves the odds that LTC premiums meaningfully contribute to deductible medical expenses, instead of being capped out prematurely. The age groups and limits for 2025 and 2026 are summarized below:

Age Group	2025 Limit	2026 Limit
40 or younger	$480	$500
41–50	$900	$930
51–60	$1,800	$1,860
61–70	$4,810	$4,960
71+	$6,020	$6,200

Why This Matters for Retirement Planning

Long-term care insurance protects against catastrophic financial risk, not minor expenses. When deductibility limits are too low, they discourage coverage precisely when it is most valuable.

Higher deductibility caps:

- Reduce the after-tax cost of maintaining LTC coverage
- Make it easier for premiums to help clear the 7.5% AGI medical deduction threshold
- Improve the long-term economics of protecting assets and independence

Granted, this doesn't eliminate the medical deduction hurdle, but it makes it far more achievable.

Example: Meet George and Laura: George is 72, and Laura is 69. They pay $14,500 per year for a qualified long-term care insurance policy.

Under prior IRS limits (2025):

- **George (72).** Up to $6,020 allowed toward medical expenses

- **Laura (69).** Up to $4,810 allowed toward medical expenses
- **Total allowed toward medical expenses.** $10,830

That means $3,670 of premiums received no tax recognition.

Under updated IRS limits (2026):

- **George (72).** Up to $6,200 allowed toward medical expenses
- **Laura (69).** Up to $4,960 allowed toward medical expenses
- **Total allowed toward medical expenses.** $11,160

Now $3,340 of premiums receive no tax recognition.

While it may not seem like much, the higher 2026 caps allow an additional $330 of their real-world premiums to count toward deductible medical expenses, improving the after-tax cost of maintaining long-term care coverage.

And every dollar counts.

Planning Takeaway

Long-term care insurance is expensive, but modernized deductibility limits make it more financially realistic to maintain coverage later in life.

By raising the caps on deductible LTC premiums, the OBBBA strengthens one of the most important, and often overlooked, tools in retirement risk management.

Conclusion: The Golden Age of Senior Tax Planning

By the end of *Grumpy Old Men*, Max and John realize that getting older doesn't make life harder—it just makes strategy more important.

The OBBBA aligns perfectly with that philosophy. It gives seniors more tools, more flexibility, more breathing room, and far fewer reasons to grumble.

Six Essential Tax Tips on the New "Trump Accounts"

Look for the Federal Head Start ($1,000)

Children born from January 1, 2025, to December 31, 2028, automatically qualify for a one-time $1,000 federal deposit into their Trump Account.

Parents don't even need to apply. The Treasury will open these accounts automatically in 2026 unless you opt out. Because the funds are invested immediately into one of the Treasury-approved index options (*Read:* not chosen by the parent), that early $1,000 gets nearly two decades of tax-deferred growth.

New parents: Be on the lookout for IRS/Treasury notifications so you know when the account is active and invested.

TIP 30

Maximize Annual Contributions ($5,000 Limit)

Families can contribute up to $5,000 per year collectively (that includes parents, grandparents, etc.).

This limit is indexed for inflation starting after 2027. Contributions are made with after-tax dollars, but the earnings grow tax-deferred, similar to an IRA.

Since you cannot pick individual investments, all contributions are allocated across the Treasury's limited menu of low-cost index funds and ETFs with fees capped at 0.1%.

Maxing the account each year is one of the best ways to leverage long-term compounding, even with the simplified investment choices.

TIP 31

Look for a Potential Employer Match (Up to $2,500)

The OBBBA allows employers to contribute up to $2,500 per year per child on a tax-free basis to the employee.

Big note: Employer contributions count toward that same $5,000 annual cap, but they are an enormous value-add if offered.

Many employers have not finalized benefit packages for 2026, so families should proactively ask HR whether this match will be added.

TIP 32

Prepare for Taxable Withdrawals After Age 18

Trump Accounts are tax-deferred, not tax-free, and this distinction matters.

Once the child turns 18, the account legally converts into an IRA-like account. The original contributions (aka the money you put in) can be withdrawn tax-free, but all earnings are taxed at the young adult's ordinary income tax rate when withdrawn.

Withdrawals before age 18 are prohibited. Smart timing of withdrawals or Roth conversions can help minimize taxes during low-income years.

TIP 33

Expect Low-Cost, Index-Based Investments Only— No Stock Picking, No Crypto

One of the unique features of Trump Accounts is that neither the parents nor the child controls investment selection beyond choosing from a small, government-approved menu.

The Treasury Department sets the investment options, restricted to low-cost index mutual funds and ETFs tracking broad U.S. equity and bond markets.

The statutory fee cap of 0.1% is set by the OBBBA. This simplicity creates consistency, fairness, and long-term efficiency.

TIP 34

Don't Miss the Dell Foundation's $250 Seed Money (for Older Kids)

Children born before January 1, 2025—roughly age 10 and under—do not qualify for the federal $1,000 deposit.

However, the Michael & Susan Dell Foundation pledged $250 seed contributions for up to 25 million Trump Accounts in zip codes where the median income is $150,000 or less. This ensures older children get a meaningful jump-start as well. So even without the federal $1,000 seed money, these children will get a Trump Account.

Once the Dell $250 contribution is deposited, the funds, like all contributions, will be invested only in Treasury-approved index options. And parents can contribute up to the full $5,000 annual limit to these accounts as well.

Families should watch for eligibility maps and official announcements rolling out in 2026.

WHO ACTUALLY CONTROLS THE MONEY IN A TRUMP ACCOUNT?

(Hint: It's not you.)

One of the most misunderstood features of the new OBBBA Trump Accounts is who decides how the money gets invested.

Unlike a 529 plan or Uniform Transfers to Minors Act (UTMA) account, where parents have broad control, Trump Accounts operate more like the federal Thrift Savings Plan (TSP) used by government employees.

Here's what families need to know:

The Treasury Department Controls the Investment Menu

Parents and beneficiaries cannot pick individual stocks, crypto, or actively managed funds. Instead, the federal government provides a small, preapproved list of low-cost index funds and ETFs that track broad U.S. stock and bond markets.

Think: S&P 500, Total U.S. Stock Market Index, U.S. Bond Index.

Parents Can Choose Among the Available Index Funds—but That's It

You can adjust how contributions are allocated within the approved menu, but you cannot go outside it. This keeps risk moderate and fees extremely low, with a statutory fee cap of 0.1%.

Children Don't Gain Full Control at 18

Even after the account converts to an IRA-like structure at age 18:

- The child still cannot pick individual investments.
- The investment menu remains restricted to the same Treasury-approved list.
- Only withdrawals and allocations can be directed by the beneficiary.

Why Congress Locked Down the Investment Choices

Lawmakers designed Trump Accounts to be:

- Simple (no trading, no salespeople, no speculation)
- Low-cost (fee caps prevent long-term erosion)
- Fair (all kids get the same access to diversified market growth)

- Protected (no parent can accidentally day-trade away a child's federal head start)

Bottom Line for Parents

You control:

✔ Whether to contribute
✔ How much to contribute
✔ How to split contributions across the approved index funds

You *do not* control:

✘ The fund list
✘ Individual stock selection
✘ Investment risk beyond the index options provided

It's a retirement-style structure built for kids—intentionally simple, intentionally passive, intentionally durable.

This is exactly the kind of planning that's easier to do early—and much harder to fix later—which is why asking questions now matters.

Side by Side: Trump Accounts Vs. 529 Plans

Feature	Trump Account (OBBBA)	529 Plan (QTP)
Primary goal	Flexible, long-term savings for general adulthood (retirement, first home, starting a business)	Tax-advantaged savings specifically for *education expenses*
Federal tax deduction	No federal deduction for contributions	No federal deduction for contributions
State tax benefit	*None* currently offered or anticipated	*Yes*, over 30 states offer a state income tax deduction or credit for contributions

Feature	Trump Account (OBBBA)	529 Plan (QTP)
Annual contribution limit	*$5,000* (from all sources, indexed for inflation after 2027)	*None* (but gifts are subject to annual exclusion limits)
Total contribution limit	Generally capped by annual limit until age 18	Lifetime limits are very high (e.g., up to $500,000 or more, depending on the state plan)
Investment selection	*Highly restricted* to a small menu of low-cost, broad index funds or ETFs	*Limited* to options offered by the plan administrator (typically professionally managed portfolios that may offer more diversity)
Government seed money	*Yes:* $1,000 for eligible newborns (2025–2028), plus the Dell Foundation's $250 contribution for qualifying older children	*No* government seed money
Tax on earnings	*Tax-deferred* growth. Earnings are taxed as *ordinary income* upon withdrawal, similar to a traditional IRA	*Tax-free* growth and withdrawals when used for qualified education expenses (QEE)
Withdrawal age/access	*Generally prohibited* until the beneficiary reaches age 18	*No age limit*; funds can be used immediately upon deposit for K–12 expenses
K–12 expense use	*No* (withdrawals are restricted until age 18)	*Yes*, up to *$20,000 per year* (starting in 2026) for tuition, books, tutoring, and more
Noneducation use	*Highly flexible:* After age 18/conversion to IRA, funds can be used for first-time home purchases, small business start-up costs, or retirement	*Limited:* Withdrawals for non-QEE are typically subject to *income tax* on earnings plus a *10% penalty*
Account flexibility	*Rigid:* Cannot be transferred to another child/family member	*Flexible:* Can change beneficiary to another family member at any time
Roth IRA rollover	*Automatic conversion* to a traditional IRA-like account at age 18	*Permitted* (SECURE 2.0): Up to a lifetime limit of $35,000 to the beneficiary's Roth IRA, subject to rules

CHAPTER THREE

Gratitude with a Garnish

How to Keep More of Your Tips Under the OBBBA

Unlocking the Historic $25,000 Deduction While Mastering the New Reporting Rules

If you earn tips—whether you're a server, bartender, stylist, bellhop, spa technician, valet, or anyone in a service-based role—the tax rules are often confusing, inconsistent, and misunderstood.

For decades, tipped workers have been required to track, report, and pay tax on every dollar received, even when tips are cash, informal, or irregular.

The One Big Beautiful Bill Act (OBBBA) finally brings meaningful relief.

Beginning in 2025, qualifying workers could deduct up to $25,000 of tip income above the line—a first in U.S. tax history.

But this new benefit doesn't erase the long-standing requirements around tip reporting, FICA, and employer rules.

This chapter gives you the *real* rules so you can stay compliant and take advantage of every tax break available.

TIP 35

Keep a Daily Tip Record

The IRS requires you to maintain a daily record of all tips, whether received in cash, by credit card, through digital apps, or as noncash items.

This is not optional. It's the long-standing rule of tip taxation—and primary defense in case the IRS questions your numbers.

You can use IRS Form 4070A to record your tips, but there are some great apps, or that good ol' spreadsheet will work too. Just use it completely and consistently: That means include the date, amount, and source and whether the tip was shared, pooled, or retained.

TIP 36

Report Cash Tips to Your Employer Monthly

If you earn $20 or more in tips in any month at the same job, you must report that total to your employer by the tenth of the following month, accordingly to IRC 6053(a).

This report must include cash tips, charged tips distributed to you, and your net amount after tip-outs. Your employer will use this number to withhold the necessary income tax, Social Security, and Medicare tax.

If you don't report tips on time, you remain personally responsible for those taxes (aka FICA taxes) you should have paid.

Even if your employer doesn't ask for the numbers, you still must provide them.

TIP 37

New: Claim the $25,000 Tip Deduction (2025–2028)

Drum roll please!!!!

Starting in 2025, tipped workers could deduct up to $25,000 of eligible tip income as an above-the-line deduction. That means it's a pure income tax deduction because it lowers the taxable income you report to the IRS. This is a big deal for people in the service industry.

But let's be crystal clear: All tips still are fully subject to FICA taxes (Social Security and Medicare), no matter what.

So even if you deduct the first $25,000 for income tax purposes, you will still owe 7.65% FICA on those tips (or 15.3% if you are self-employed).

The new deduction does *not* remove the FICA obligations in any way.

But this new deduction is available to all taxpayers—even those who take the standard deduction—which makes it incredibly valuable for workers who rarely itemize.

It phases out, or goes away, once your income gets above $150,000 (as a single person) and $300,000 (for a couple married filing jointly) to keep the benefit focused on middle-income households.

This is the first time in U.S. history that the IRS is allowing a special income tax break specifically for tip income, a recognition that service-industry pay is volatile, unpredictable, and often underprotected.

And while again, it doesn't reduce FICA, it does lower taxable income, giving many workers their first meaningful tax relief in decades (OBBBA section 224).

WHAT "ABOVE THE LINE" REALLY MEANS

An *above-the-line deduction* is one taken before your adjusted gross income is calculated. This is super important because AGI affects tons of tax thresholds, credits, and deductions. Unlike itemized deductions, above-the-line deductions benefit every taxpayer, whether or not they itemize.

Lowering your AGI can also improve your eligibility for tax credits and retirement contributions and even reduce Medicare premiums later in life. For tipped workers, this new deduction provides real financial relief and is far more powerful than a typical below-the-line write-off.

We definitely need an example here: Let's say in 2025 you earn *$40,000 in tips* for the year.

Step 1: Apply the new deduction

You can deduct $25,000 of those tips as an above-the-line deduction.

So for income tax purposes, the IRS will tax you on $15,000:

$$40{,}000 - \$25{,}000 = \$15{,}000 \text{ of tip income}$$

This lowers your taxable income and could save you tons of money, depending on your tax bracket.

Step 2: FICA still applies to the full amount

Even though you're only taxed on $15,000 for income tax, you must still pay FICA on the entire $40,000.

That means you owe:

- *7.65%* if you are an employee and you told your employer about all your tips
- *15.3%* if you are self-employed

So FICA is calculated on the full $40,000, not the reduced $15,000.

Step 3: Your tax bill goes down, not your payroll tax

Remember, this deduction won't change your Social Security or Medicare tax bill, but it can significantly reduce what you owe when filing your return, especially if you normally take the standard deduction.

TIP 38

Tips Are Still Subject to FICA (Always Have Been)

This is worth repeating.

Even with the new deduction, all tips remain fully subject to Social Security and Medicare taxes. Nothing in the OBBBA changes this. So if you earn $10,000 in tips, you owe FICA tax on the full $10,000.

Period. End of story.

Many workers mistakenly believe cash tips escape tax, but that's never been true; FICA applies regardless of whether the tips were reported on time or not (IRC 3101, 3111).

TIP 39

For Tip Pools, Only Report Your Net Tips

When tip-sharing or pooling is involved, you only report the amount you actually keep, not the amount initially received. For example, if you received $400 in tips but tipped out $100 to bussers and bartenders, your reportable amount is $300.

Keeping documentation of tip-outs is crucial, because the IRS wants to see that the reduction is legitimate and part of a recognized pooling arrangement.

Don't forget to do this, or you indirectly will increase your taxable income—and then you'll owe more tax.

TIP 40

Understand "Uncollected FICA" on Your W-2

If your paycheck isn't large enough for your employer to withhold all required FICA taxes on your reported tips, the unpaid amount is listed on your W-2 in Box 12 with Code A or B.

This isn't a mistake—it's a record of taxes that you still owe.

You must pay these uncollected taxes when filing your Form 1040.

Failing to do so can result in penalties and interest, and the IRS can assess the difference years later.

This situation unfortunately is common in restaurants, salons, and spas where base wages are low.

TIP 41

Report *All* Tips on Your 1040 (Even Noncash)

Every tip you receive—cash, Venmo, credit card, gift card, tickets, wine bottles, or even holiday gifts—technically is taxable income, according to IRC 61(a).

The IRS expects you to report the *fair market value* of any noncash item received as a tip.

Even if you didn't report the tips to your employer, you must still include them on your tax return. Failure to report noncash tips is a common audit trigger in service industries.

Transparency is key here—plus, you're protecting your future Social Security benefits.

TIP 42

Pay Self-Employment Tax on Unreported Tips

If you earned $20 or more in cash tips in a month and did not report them to your employer, you must pay the *full 15.3%* in FICA taxes yourself—that means both the employer and employee portions.

You can use Form 4137 to do this yourself and include it with your tax return.

Again, back to the FICA rules—the IRS does not want you to avoid paying FICA. So not reporting your tips to your employer doesn't reduce your tax burden; it increases it.

TIP 43

Verify Allocated Tips on Your W-2

Okay, first—what the heck are "allocated tips"?

Allocated tips are the amounts your employer must report to the IRS, and they show up in Box 8 of your W-2.

If you work at a large restaurant (typically one with more than 10 employees), the IRS assumes total tips should equal at least 8% of the restaurant's gross sales.

If the total tips reported by all employees combined fall below this 8% threshold, your employer is required to allocate the difference among the staff. This allocated amount appears in your Box 8.

But here's the problem: Allocated tips are income that is allocated to you but *zero* taxes have been withheld.

And the IRS basically says, "We believe you earned this income, and now you owe all the taxes on it."

So be sure to check out Box 8 on your W-2 and make sure you are paying tax on that money.

TIP 44

Self-Employed Workers Can Claim the $25,000 Tip Deduction

Independent contractors such as stylists, nail techs, massage therapists, rideshare drivers, and aestheticians can also claim the new tip deduction.

But again, you must still pay full self-employment tax on tip income, just as you do for all business income.

The deduction reduces taxable income but does not reduce self-employment tax obligations, as we have discussed.

Self-employed workers should keep detailed logs because there is no employer to help with withholding or reporting.

This deduction gives entrepreneurs in service fields a rare opportunity to lower their taxable income, though.

The Five Additional Facts Most People Miss

TIP 45

Electronic Tips (Venmo, Zelle, Cash App) Are Fully Taxable

Digital tips may feel informal, but they are treated just like cash tips for tax purposes.

Even if the payment app does not issue a 1099-K (as discussed in Tip 99), the income is still fully taxable.

The IRS increasingly monitors digital transactions and expects accurate reporting, regardless of platform.

So keep screenshots or monthly summaries to substantiate the amounts you received.

TIP 46

IRS Tip Monitoring Is Increasing Under OBBBA

The IRS now has stronger technological tools, more POS data, and higher transparency from digital payment systems.

Under OBBBA, enhanced matching programs compare sales, reported tips, and typical industry percentages. If reported tips consistently appear too low, the IRS may send inquiries or propose adjustments.

This doesn't mean you should panic—it means you need to be prepared. So keep good records.

TIP 47

Service Charges Are Not Tips

A mandatory "service fee" (such as 18% for large parties) is considered wage income under IRS rules, not a tip.

That means the employer must withhold tax on it, and workers have no flexibility to treat it as tip income.

Many customers mistakenly believe they are tipping when they pay a service fee, but legally, it's not a tip.

This distinction is critical for accurate reporting and for avoiding misunderstandings about taxable income. Always clarify whether a charge is a true tip or a service fee.

Quick example: A restaurant adds an automatic 20% service fee to a $200 check.

The customer thinks he's tipping $40. But the IRS says, "Nope. That's not a tip to the server. That is part of his wages." All because it is listed on the receipt as a "service fee."

The $40 goes to the employee as W-2 wages, and the employer must withhold taxes:

- Employee pays tax on the $40.
- Employer pays the payroll-tax share on the $40.

The customer's intention or generosity doesn't matter here—the IRS's classification does.

TIP 48

States May Not Follow the Federal Deduction

The new $25,000 federal tip deduction applies only at the federal level unless a state chooses to conform.

Some states mirror federal tax law, others do not, and a few selectively adopt provisions. Workers in high-tax states should pay special attention to their state's position to avoid surprises at filing time.

The difference between federal and state treatment may affect withholding decisions. As guidance evolves, staying updated can prevent costly state-level underpayments.

So it's important you check with your state.

TIP 49

Keep Separate Logs if You Work Multiple Jobs

Tip reporting rules apply separately for each employer.

If you work at two restaurants and earn $20 in tips at each, you must report tips to each employer individually.

So keep separate logs to avoid confusion, misreporting, and potential underpayment penalties.

This becomes especially important if one employer uses tip pooling systems and the other does not.

Tipped workers form the backbone of the service economy, and tax law is finally offering a measure of relief.

The new $25,000 deduction is historic and wonderful—but it works only when there is documentation to back it all. With accurate records, timely reporting, and thoughtful planning, service workers can dramatically reduce their tax burden and stay fully compliant.

So treat those tip logs and tax records as important tools that protect your income and your financial future. You work really hard serving people (especially the not-so-nice ones), so you deserve to keep as much of that hard-earned money as you can.

CHAPTER FOUR

The Family Fortune

20 Ways to Build a Tax-Smart Legacy for Your Inner Circle

Unlocking Kid Credits, Education Wins, and the New OBBBA "Trump Account" Revolution

Family Tax Tips—20 Ways to Keep More
in Your Family's Pocket

Family life is wonderful—and really expensive sometimes. Between childcare, college savings, healthcare, and that constantly increasing grocery bill, every dollar counts. The good news is that Uncle Sam (semi) understands and offers a bunch of ways to give you a break—if you know where to look.

Remember—there's a big difference between tax credits and deductions. A *tax credit* is a dollar-for-dollar reduction of your final tax bill, so way more bang for your buck.

A *tax deduction* reduces your taxable income based on your tax bracket, so you may only get a percentage of the deducted amount depending on how much you earn.

So let's talk credits first.

Kid Credits

TIP 50

Child Tax Credit

If you have kids under 17, you could qualify for up to $2,000 per child with the Child Tax Credit. It phases out for higher earners, but many middle-income families still qualify. Even if you owe little or no tax, a portion of the credit still can get you some cash back.

TIP 51

Child and Dependent Care (CDC) Credit

It's available to taxpayers who pay for the care of a "qualifying person" (which typically is a dependent child under age 13 or a disabled spouse/dependent) to enable the taxpayer (and spouse if married) to work or actively look for work.

To claim the credit, you must have earned income and file as single, head of household, or married filing jointly. It covers up to a maximum of $6,000 for two or more dependents.

It covers expenses for services necessary to take care of the qualifying person while the taxpayer (and spouse if married) works or searches for work. So that's stuff like daycare, preschool, day camps (not sleepaway!), babysitters, nannies, and *all* those after-school programs.

TIP 52

Earned Income Tax Credit (EITC)

This is a big deal for low- to moderate-income working families, worth up to $7,830 in 2025 for households with three or more children. It's refundable, meaning you can get money back even if you don't owe taxes.

TIP 53

Adoption Credit

You can claim up to $16,810 per child in 2025 for adoption-related expenses like legal fees, travel, and agency costs. The credit can carry forward for up to five years. You deserve it. You're doing a beautiful thing.

Education Credits (AOTC and LLC)

TIP 54

The American Opportunity Tax Credit (AOTC)

The AOTC is worth up to $2,500 per eligible student for the first four years of college.

It's one of the most generous tax breaks for higher education expenses, providing up to $2,500 per eligible student for the first four years of college.

It's calculated by taking 100% of the first $2,000 in qualified expenses and 25% of the next $2,000 in qualified expenses.

Even better, up to $1,000 is refundable, meaning you can receive cash back even if the credit reduces your tax liability to zero.

TIP 55

The Lifetime Learning Credit (LLC)

The LLC offers up to $2,000 to help cover qualified tuition and fees for eligible educational institutions. Unlike the AOTC, the LLC can be claimed for any level of postsecondary education, including undergraduate, graduate, or professional development courses, and there is no limit to the number of years it can be claimed, which is great for the overachievers in your family.

But the LLC can only reduce your tax bill to zero; you *can't* get a refund from it like you can from the AOTC.

The credit is calculated at 20% of the first $10,000 in educational expenses and is subject to income phaseouts.

Now the Deductions

TIP 56

Deduct Student Loan Interest

You may be able to deduct up to $2,500 of interest paid each year. Even if you cosigned the loan and your child makes the payments, if you are legally obligated to pay the debt, you can take the deduction.

Even better, you don't need to itemize your deductions to get the benefit.

TIP 57

Deduct Medical Expenses for Dependents

This deduction usually is tough to qualify for, but if you have a bunch of out-of-pocket medical expenses, it's worth tallying up.

To start, you need to itemize your deductions. If you don't, move on.

If you do itemize, you can deduct medical expenses for yourself and dependents, even adult children you still support, as long as the expenses are *greater* than 7.5% of your adjusted gross income (AGI). Therein lies the issue. This could be a tough number to hit.

Quick example: If your AGI is $100,000, your expenses must *exceed* $7,500 (7.5%). Then only the amount that exceeds is deductible. So if you have $8,000 in out-of-pocket expenses, you will get to deduct $500 in this example.

TIP 58
Deduct Charitable Driving Mileage

If you or your kids volunteer for a qualified charity, things like driving for a school fundraiser, the Boy Scouts, or your church, you can deduct your mileage at a flat rate of 14 cents per mile for 2025.

This small deduction is often missed, but if you have kids and play the role of their Uber on the regular, start keeping track.

TIP 59
Use That Dependent Care Account with Your Flexible Spending Account (FSA)

If you have an FSA at work, use it to pay up to $5,000 per year in eligible childcare costs.

Day camps (but not overnight camps) often qualify, so keep those receipts!

Just know that if you use your dependent care credit to pay for one of your kid's day camps, you can't use that same expense against the CDC credit. No double counting.

TIP 60
Beef Up Your Health Savings Account (HSA) — It's a Triple Tax Advantage Tool

If you have a high-deductible health plan (HDHP) at work, contributions to an HSA are tax-deductible. Even better, those contributions grow tax-free, and withdrawals, used for qualified medical expenses, also are tax-free.

So ask your employer if an HSA is an option for you (see Chapter Eleven for more details).

For 2025, the family contribution limit is $8,550.

TIP 61

Take Advantage of the Newborn Savings Account (One Big Beautiful Bill Act Update)

As we mentioned in Chapter Two, the Big Beautiful Bill introduced Newborn Savings Accounts, or Trump Accounts, available for children born in the United States after 2025.

The account is opened with a $1,000 federal deposit if the parents elect it (so elect it!), and outside contributions can be made up to a $5,000 annual limit. These accounts work like 529 plans, growing tax-free for education or other qualified uses

The money generally cannot be accessed until the kid turns 18, after which it functions like a traditional IRA with penalty-free withdrawals for purposes such as higher education or a first-time home purchase.

TIP 62

Save for College (and *Way* More) with a 529 Plan

529 plans are a powerful way to save for education. Earnings grow tax-free, and withdrawals are tax-free for qualified expenses like tuition, books, room and board, and those laptops. But it's more than college. They cover everything from K–12 private school tuition (up to $10,000 per year) to costs at trade schools and graduate programs.

Ideally, you start funding one as soon as the baby is born.

TIP 63

Use 529 Funds for Student Loan Repayment

You can use funds from a 529 plan to pay principal and interest on student loans up to a $10,000 lifetime limit per individual (beneficiary and siblings), thanks to the Setting Every Community Up for Retirement Enhancement (SECURE) Act of 2019.

This is a great way to use leftover funds tax-free, if you actually have any.

Child Employment and Retirement

TIP 64

Put Your Kids on the Payroll

If you own a business, especially a sole proprietorship or parent-owned partnership, wages paid to your child for legitimate work are deductible to you and often tax-free to them if they earn less than the standard deduction, which is $14,600 for 2025.

Even better, you don't have to withhold Social Security or Medicare taxes for kids under 18.

TIP 65

Fund a Roth IRA for Your Child—The Ultimate Head Start

Once your kid has earned income, from your business, babysitting, etc., your kid can open a Roth IRA. Contributions, up to $7,000 for 2025, grow and are withdrawn tax-free in retirement.

Parents can fund the account on the child's behalf up to the amount the child actually earned.

TIP 66

Use the Annual Gift Tax Exclusion

You can gift up to $18,000 per person per year for 2025 to as many people as you want without touching your lifetime exemption. A married couple can give $36,000 per child tax-free each year.

Note that paying tuition or medical bills directly to the institution or provider does not count toward this limit.

TIP 67

Understand the "Kiddie Tax" Rule

Be careful when gifting assets that generate passive income, like interest, dividends, or capital gains.

In 2025, unearned income above $2,700 is taxed at the *parents'* marginal tax rate.

To avoid this, focus on funding Roth IRAs, which grow tax-free, rather than taxable custodial accounts.

This stuff gets tricky, so be sure to talk to your accountant.

Filing Status

TIP 68

File as Head of Household (HOH) if You Qualify

If you're single and paying more than half the cost of keeping up a home for a qualifying dependent, HOH offers a higher standard deduction and lower tax brackets than filing as single.

Divorced women, in particular, are quick to check "Single" when filling out their returns, but the HOH is much more beneficial if you qualify.

TIP 69

Check for Qualifying Widow(er) Status

If your spouse passed away recently and you have a dependent child, you may be able to use the Qualifying Widow(er) filing status for two years after the year of death.

This allows you to still use the favorable joint return tax rates and the highest standard deduction.

Bonus: Keep Family Finances Current, and Complete at Least an Annual Review

Families constantly evolve. Review beneficiaries, wills, insurance policies, and, most importantly, your tax withholding (W-4) every year, especially after major life events like marriage, divorce, a new child, or a job change.

CHAPTER FIVE

The Shelter Strategy

Maximizing Your Home as a Tax Shield Under the OBBBA

Mastering the $40,000 SALT Break, the PMI Comeback, and the "Money Pit" Protection Plan

Homeownership is an amazing asset and remains one of the greatest tax shelters available.

But anyone who saw one of my favorite movies, *The Money Pit*, starring Tom Hanks and Shelley Long, from 1986, knows that it could also be exceptionally costly.

You need to itemize your deductions to get many of the benefits. The Tax Cuts and Jobs Act (TCJA) and the subsequent One Big Beautiful Bill Act (OBBBA) raised the standard deduction and definitely reduced the number of people who can itemize; for those that still do, the benefits are significant.

Major Deductions and OBBBA Updates

TIP 70

Exploit the Expanded SALT Deduction (OBBBA Update)

The deduction for state and local taxes (SALT), which includes property taxes, was capped at $10,000 under the TCJA.

The OBBBA temporarily raises to $40,000 ($20,000 for married filing separately) for tax years 2025 through 2029 for most taxpayers. So take advantage while you can.

This is a massive, albeit short-lived, break for homeowners in high-tax states, like for me in New Jersey.

TIP 71

Deduct Mortgage Interest

You can deduct interest paid on a mortgage used to buy, build, or substantially improve your home up to $750,000 ($375,000 if married filing separately) for loans taken out after December 15, 2017.

The OBBBA unfortunately made this limit permanent.

TIP 72

Don't Forget to Use the $1 Million Limit on Grandfathered Loans

If your mortgage was secured on or before December 15, 2017, you are "grandfathered" in under the older, higher limit and can deduct interest to $1 million ($500,000 if married filing separately).

Any mortgage after that goes back to Tip 70 rules.

TIP 73

Use HELOC Interest for Home Improvement Only

Interest on a Home Equity Line of Credit (HELOC) or second mortgage is only deductible if the funds are used to buy, build, or substantially improve the home that secures the debt.

If the money is used for personal expenses, like college tuition or that long-awaited trip around the world, the interest is not deductible. (Doesn't mean you shouldn't take the trip, though.)

TIP 74

Deduct Property Taxes Paid

You can deduct real estate taxes paid on all your properties—that includes your primary residence and vacation home, up to the overall SALT limit, which currently is $40,000, thanks to the OBBBA, for 2025–2029.

We will discuss rental properties in Chapter Six.

TIP 75

Deduct Private Mortgage Insurance (PMI) Premiums Again (Starting 2026)

The OBBBA allows you to deduct PMI premiums beginning in tax year 2026 if you itemize your deductions.

This deduction is back from 2021. It is subject to income phaseouts, starting at $100,000 AGI for most filers, but is a major win for first-time buyers who put down less than 20%.

Maximizing Closing Cost and Refinance Deductions

TIP 76

Deduct Mortgage Points on Purchase

Points paid when you purchase a home are generally treated as prepaid interest and are usually fully deductible in the year they are paid, provided they are customary for your area.

Again, you have to itemize your deductions to qualify.

If the seller paid points on your behalf, you still can deduct them, but you must reduce the cost basis of your home by the amount of those points. Talk to your accountant here.

TIP 77

Deduct Property Taxes Paid at Closing

Do not miss the property taxes you reimbursed the seller for at closing. This amount is shown on your settlement sheet (Closing Disclosure) and is deductible in the year of purchase, again subject to the overall SALT limit, and again you have to itemize your deductions to qualify.

And note that the buyer and seller only can deduct the property taxes for the portion of the year that they owned the home. So the deduction must be split regardless of who wrote the check at closing.

TIP 78

Amortize Refinance Points over the Loan Life

Unlike points on a new mortgage, if you pay points when refinancing your mortgage, you cannot deduct them all at once.

Instead, you must deduct (the accountants say "amortize") them ratably over the life of the new loan.

TIP 79

Fully Deduct Prior Refi Points on Sale/Payoff

If you had a prior mortgage loan that had points you were amortizing and you paid the loan off with a second refinance or sale, the remaining undeducted points from the *first* refinance can be fully deducted in the year the loan is paid off.

So be sure to keep track of all this stuff.

TIP 80

Add Most Closing Costs to Your Home's Basis

Most other closing costs—like title insurance, appraisal fees, attorney fees, recording fees, and transfer taxes—are not immediately deductible.

Instead, add them to your cost basis, or original purchase price of the home. This is super important because a higher cost basis reduces your taxable profit when you eventually sell the home.

See Tip 85 for more details.

TIP 81

Deduct Interest Paid Before Closing

Tons of people miss this, but any interest you pay on your mortgage from the date of closing, up to the end of the month, is considered prepaid interest and is fully deductible in the year you close.

Again, you must itemize.

TIP 82

Deduct EV Charger Installation Costs (Alternative Fuel Refueling Property Credit)

If you install an electric vehicle charger at your home, you can get a credit for up to 30% of the cost, maxed out at $1,000.

Note that this credit is available for property placed in service before June 30, 2026.

Advanced Strategies and Planning

TIP 83

Maximize the Home Sale Exclusion to Minimize Your Capital Gains at Sale

When you sell your primary residence, you can exclude a certain percentage of the profit from taxable income—

- Up to $250,000, as a single person

  or
- Up to $500,000 as a married couple filing jointly

if you pass the following tests:

The Ownership and Use Tests

1. You must have owned the home for at least two years.
2. You must have lived in that home as your principal residence for at least two years during the five-year period ending on the date of the sale.

Neither the ownership nor the use period needs to be continuous, but both must add up to 24 months total within that 5-year window.

So if you pass both tests and your total gain on the sale of your home is $50,000, you pay no capital gains tax to Uncle Sam. Wahoo!

But if your gain is $275,000 as a single person, you will owe capital gains tax on $25,000 ($275,000 − $250,000).

Big note: You can only claim this full exclusion once every two years.

A partial exclusion may be available if you are forced to sell early due to qualified health, employment, or unforeseen circumstances. Read on.

TIP 84

Claim a Partial Home Sale Exclusion

If you are forced to sell your home before meeting the two-year test due to unforeseen circumstances, like a job loss, divorce, health issues, or a pregnancy resulting in multiple births (that means twins or more!), you may still qualify for a partial exclusion of the gain based on the time you lived there.

Talk to your accountant.

TIP 85

Keep Receipts to Increase Your Home's "Basis"

"Basis" is a wonky word for the purchase price of your home plus any fees or commissions.

But the higher your "basis," the lower your tax bill when it comes time to sell. So be sure to add the cost of capital improvements, like adding a room, replacing the roof, or remodeling the kitchen, to your basis.

We need a quick example here: Let's say you bought a home for $100,000 and sold it for $150,000.

In very simple terms, you may have a $50,000 capital gain here, depending on whether you meet the home sale exclusion rules discussed in Tip 84. But if you put in a $20,000 kitchen, you need to add that to the basis. Now the basis is $120,000. If you still sell for $150,000, your capital gain is now only $30,000.

See? Less tax to Uncle Sam.

It's super important to keep detailed records of these improvements in case anyone ever asks for proof.

TIP 86

Deduct Medically Necessary Home Improvements (Itemized Deduction)

If you install home improvements primarily for medical care, like a wheelchair ramp or specialized railings, and the main purpose is medical care for you, your spouse, or a dependent—not to increase the value of the house—you may be able to include the cost as an itemized medical expense.

As a reminder, you have to itemize, and the total medical costs you are deducting must exceed 7.5% of your adjusted gross income.

I know, not easy.

TIP 87

Convert a Rental to a Primary Residence (for Exclusion)

If you sell an investment property, you are subject to capital gains tax.

However, if you convert the rental to your primary residence and live there for at least two years before selling it, you can take advantage of the $250,000/$500,000 home sale exclusion we talked about in Tip 83.

Talk to your accountant about this one because you have to pay attention to depreciation amounts, which can get wonky, but don't leave this option on the table either.

Whew, that was a lot. But so is your house. It can be exhausting and expensive.

I love Tom Hanks's famous line in *The Money Pit*: "Here lies Walter Fielding. He bought a house . . . and it killed him."

Be smarter than Walter. At least get some money back on your tax return.

CHAPTER SIX

The Rental Playbook

Tax Hacks to Turn Your Property into a Wealth-Building Machine

Mastering the 14-Day Loophole, the "Phantom" Deduction, and the OBBBA Wins

Running an Airbnb isn't exactly *The Holiday*—mainly because there's no guarantee your guests will look like Jude Law or Cameron Diaz.

But it can still be pretty rewarding when your tax strategy is dialed in.

So whether you're renting out a vacation home, managing a long-term tenant, or listing your spare room on Airbnb, your rental income deserves to work as hard as you do.

The good news is that the U.S. tax code is surprisingly friendly to property owners who understand the rules. From depreciation, aka the ultimate "phantom deduction," to the 14-day tax-free rental loophole, there are dozens of legitimate ways to reduce what you owe and boost what you keep.

TIP 88

Use the 14-Day Rental Loophole (IRC § 280A)

This is one of the best-kept secrets in the tax code.

Under Section 280A(g), you can rent out your personal home for up to 14 days per year and pay *zero* federal income tax on that rental income. That also means you don't even have to report it.

That means if your city hosts a big event, like the Super Bowl, and you rent out your place for a premium, it's completely tax-free. The only condition is that you can't claim any deductions related to those days.

That means no cleaning fees, supplies, or repairs for those 14 days.

The key is to stay under 15 days, because even one extra day blows it and you will have to pay tax on the full amount.

Definitely keep good records here.

TIP 89

Deduct All "Ordinary and Necessary" Expenses (IRC § 162)

Running your rental like a business means you get to deduct legitimate business expenses, and you can cast a pretty wide net here.

Under Section 162(a), you can deduct anything that's "ordinary and necessary" for managing or maintaining your rental property.

So that includes utilities, insurance, cleaning, maintenance, and even professional services. Every dollar you deduct directly reduces your taxable profit, and that's money you keep in your pocket.

Good recordkeeping is everything. Track receipts, invoices, and mileage if you drive to check on your property. Basically, if it's a real cost that helps you earn rent, it's probably deductible.

Where Do You Report All of This?

TIP 90

Use Schedule C for Active Airbnb Hosting (IRC § 1402)

If you're hands-on with your short-term rental—meaning you go beyond simply renting space and begin providing hotel-style guest services—the IRS may treat your Airbnb activity as a trade or business, rather than passive rental income.

Basic hosting tasks such as greeting guests, supplying clean towels, and cleaning between stays are typically considered normal rental activity. However, when you provide substantial services primarily for the guest's convenience—such as meals, regular housekeeping during the stay, transportation, or concierge-style experiences—your operation begins to resemble a hospitality business.

In those cases, income and expenses may need to be reported on Schedule C, similar to other small-business owners, instead of Schedule E.

The downside is that profits may be subject to self-employment tax for Social Security and Medicare, depending on the level of services provided under IRC §1402(a)-4.

There can also be an upside: if you materially participate and meet applicable requirements, losses may be able to offset other income, such as wages or consulting income, particularly in early years when setup and furnishing costs are high.

TIP 91

Use Schedule E for Long-Term Rentals (IRC § 469)

If, on the other hand, your rental is more of a passive investment, meaning tenants stay for months and you don't provide daily services to them, then you'll file on Schedule E instead.

The good news here is that this income isn't subject to self-employment tax, so that saves the 15.3%.

The trade-off is that your losses usually fall under "passive activity loss" rules, meaning they can only offset other passive income.

This stuff gets wonky, but basically, if you don't have other rental properties or other passive income sources, those losses may get "suspended" until you sell the property.

They're not lost though. They just carry forward until you sell or have offsetting income.

TIP 92

Separate Taxes for Business Use (IRC § 164)

Here's where many hosts miss out: Property taxes for your rental are not subject to the $10,000 SALT cap.

Under Section 164, you can deduct 100% of the portion related to your rental property as a business expense. That's a big deal if you live in a high-tax state where your personal deductions are maxed out.

You just have to split the personal and rental portions correctly if it's a shared property.

The tax jargon says the business share is an "above-the-line" deduction. That just means it lowers your adjusted gross income.

But it's worth taking the time to calculate the split properly or have your accountant do it.

TIP 93

Build Wealth Using Depreciation: The "Phantom Deduction" (IRC § 167)

Depreciation is one of the smartest ways real estate investors quietly build wealth. So first, let's define "depreciation."

Depreciation is how the IRS lets you write off the gradual wear and tear of your rental property over time, even if you didn't spend any cash on it that year. For residential real estate, you can deduct a portion of your building's value each year for 27.5 years.

We definitely need an example: Let's say your rental property (excluding the land) is worth $275,000. The IRS lets you divide that over 27.5 years. So that means you can deduct $10,000 a year as depreciation, even if you didn't spend a penny in repairs.

That's $10,000 off your taxable income every single year, just for owning the property.

So this deduction lowers your taxable income without lowering your actual cash flow, which is why it's often called a "phantom" deduction.

Just remember, land doesn't depreciate; only the building and qualifying improvements do.

TIP 94

Deduct Costs of Attracting Guests (IRC § 162)

Making your property more appealing isn't just good business; it's tax-deductible too.

Section 162 also allows you to write off the "ordinary and necessary" expenses you incur to attract guests.

This includes professional cleaning, decor upgrades, photography, and even fresh linens or toiletries that elevate the guest experience, like that lavender bubble bath.

The differentiator here is that these items must be directly related to the rental business, not your personal enjoyment.

But let's face it: A beautifully presented property commands higher rates *and* earns a better tax return—that's clearly good business.

TIP 95

Deduct Travel Expenses for Rental Business (IRC § 162)

Traveling to check on or manage your rental can count as a business expense if you do it the right way.

Section 162 allows deductions for travel directly tied to your rental activity.

So if you have to get on a plane to inspect the property, meet with contractors, or handle emergencies, then you can include airfare, lodging, rental cars, and even 50% of meals when they're business-related.

Big note: If you mix business with pleasure (say, a family vacation with a stop at your rental), you'll need to allocate only the business portion.

TIP 96

Move Personal Home Deductions to Your Rental (IRC § 280A)

If you rent out part of your home—like a basement or guest suite—you can shift a portion of your home expenses to that rental.

Section 280A lets you allocate costs based on square footage or time used for business versus personal purposes.

That means part of your mortgage interest, utilities, and property taxes can move from itemized deductions (which are capped) to business deductions (which aren't).

This simple reclassification can open up meaningful tax savings, especially if you live in a high-cost area.

The key is keeping good records of how much space and time your rental is used. It's worth maybe even sketching a floor plan or keeping photos to support your math.

With a few calculations, that spare room can work just as hard for you as your tenants do for rent.

TIP 97

Account for Escrow Taxes on HUD-1 (IRC § 164)

When you buy or sell a property, the closing statement (HUD-1 or settlement sheet) tells you exactly how the property taxes were split between buyer and seller.

We talked about this in Tip 77—home sale:

- If you reimbursed the seller for prepaid taxes, that amount becomes your deduction.
- If the buyer covered part of your share, you lose that portion of the write-off.

It's an easy detail to miss, but an important one to get right when your tax preparer asks for the numbers.

And then keep the HUD-1 in your permanent records; it's a key tax document, not just a closing form.

TIP 98

Issue Form 1099-MISC for Service Providers (IRC § 6041)

If you hire anyone who isn't a corporation—like a handyman, cleaner, or landscaper—and you pay them *$600 or more* during the year, the IRS expects you to send them a Form 1099-MISC.

Section 6041 requires it, and skipping this step can trigger penalties or jeopardize your deductions.

The good news? It's easy to stay compliant.

Before you pay anyone, have them fill out Form W-9 to collect their Tax ID number. Then file the 1099 by the January deadline.

Doing it right lets the IRS know that you are running your rental like a real business. A quick bit of paperwork now saves big headaches later.

TIP 99

But—You Can Avoid Issuing 1099-MISC with Credit Card Payments (IRC § 6050W)

Want to cut down on the above tax paperwork?

Pay your contractors with a credit card or qualifying online payment processor instead of a paper check. Under Section 6050W, the IRS shifts the reporting burden to the payment processor. So the processor will issue a Form 1099-K to your contractor, and then you don't have to send a Form 1099-MISC.

Platforms that qualify include major credit cards (Visa, Mastercard, Amex, Discover) and third-party processors, such as PayPal Goods & Services, Stripe, Square, and Shopify Payments.

Big note: Always choose the business-class option ("Goods & Services") when paying through a platform. It may cost a small processing fee, but it keeps your records clean and compliant and saves you from having to issue 1099-MISC forms later.

Platforms that generally do NOT qualify: Peer-to-peer apps used for personal transfers, such as Venmo (friends and family) or Cash App (personal). Big note, Zelle does not issue 1099-Ks because it is a direct bank-to-bank transfer. If you pay a contractor via Zelle, you are still responsible for issuing the 1099-NEC.

Just make sure your transactions are clearly marked as business payments (for example, "PayPal Goods & Services," not "Friends & Family").

As always—keep good records.

Now a Few Good Deductions Folks with Rental Properties Often Forget

TIP 100

Deduct Interest on Time-Shares (IRC § 163)

If you own a time-share and use it as a personal vacation spot, you may still be able to deduct the mortgage interest.

Section 163(h) allows the deduction as long as it qualifies as a "second home."

The big rule is that you must personally use it for more than 14 days or 10% of the total rental days per year. That keeps it in "personal residence" status for tax purposes.

While time-shares can be tricky, this deduction can help offset part of your ownership costs. Just be sure you don't double-dip by claiming it as both a personal and rental property. If you do rent it occasionally, track those days separately so you don't lose your eligibility.

TIP 101

Depreciate Qualified Improvements (IRC § 168)

If you've remodeled your rental—for instance, you upgraded lighting, replaced flooring, or renovated bathrooms—that may qualify as qualified improvement property under Section 168.

The IRS now lets you depreciate those improvements over 15 years instead of 39, which means faster deductions.

It's a great way to recover your investment sooner and improve cash flow. Some improvements even qualify for bonus depreciation, which can let you deduct the full cost immediately.

Things like new walls or HVAC systems probably count, but a full-blown addition does not.

The rules here change all the time, so talk to you accountant.

TIP 102

Deduct Interest to Private Lenders (IRC § 6050H)

Did you have to borrow money from a friend, family member, or private investor to buy a rental property?

Section 6050H says you can deduct the mortgage interest you paid to them, just like you would with a bank loan. But here you need to report the lender's Tax ID to the IRS.

That lets the IRS match your deduction to the lender's reported income.

Keep your signed loan agreements and payment records on file.

Just treat your "private" loan like a real loan, and you'll be able to enjoy the same tax benefits as if you borrowed from a big bank.

TIP 103

Prove Your Profit Motive (IRC § 183)

Remember, the IRS draws a sharp line between hobbies and businesses.

If your rental shows losses year after year, Section 183 allows the IRS to reclassify it as a "hobby," and that means you do not get any of these deductions. So if you want to maximize the tax code, act like a professional landlord and treat your rental as a business.

Keep detailed books, advertise vacancies, adjust rent to market rates, and track every expense.

Even if you're not profitable every year, showing that you *intend* to make a profit is what matters.

A written business plan or annual review can be your best defense.

The IRS doesn't require you to win every year—it just needs to know you're trying to.

TIP 104

Understand Local Hotel/Lodging Taxes (State/Local Law)

Airbnb hosts often forget that short-term rentals are still subject to local lodging or occupancy taxes.

These are sometimes called "hotel taxes" or "transient occupancy taxes," and they're imposed at the city or county level. No matter what they are called, ignoring them can lead to steep fees.

The good news is that many platforms like Airbnb and Vrbo automatically collect and remit these taxes for you—just not always.

So check your city's website or call the finance department to clarify.

TIP 105

Deposit Refinance Funds into a Business Account (IRC § 163)

If you pull cash out from refinancing your personal home to buy or improve a rental, the IRS wants to see a clean paper trail. Under Section 163, you can only deduct the interest on that borrowed money if it's clearly tied to business use.

The easiest way to prove that is to deposit the refinance proceeds directly into your rental's *separate* business account.

If you mix the funds with personal money, it becomes nearly impossible to trace—and you could lose the deduction.

Keep copies of bank transfers, loan documents, and receipts for how the funds were used. This small step establishes a solid "business purpose" trail.

TIP 106

Report Unpaid Interest from Loans (IRC § 446)

Under Section 446, you can only deduct interest once it's *actually paid*. Now this is a subtle—but important—rule.

It means if your loan accrues unpaid interest that's added to the balance (the accountants call that "negative amortization"), you can't deduct it yet.

The deduction comes later, when you eventually pay that interest in full. This is common in adjustable-rate or balloon loans, so check your statements carefully.

And be sure to keep track so you don't double count the interest.

TIP 107

Understand Passive Activity Loss Limitations (IRC § 469)

Most rental losses fall under the passive activity loss (PAL) rules in Section 469.

That means you generally can't use those losses to offset wages or other active income. But there's an exception: If you "actively participate" in the rental—meaning you make key management decisions—and your income is under $100,000, you can deduct up to $25,000 in losses.

That's a huge tax break for middle-income investors.

Now once your modified adjusted gross income passes $150,000, the deduction phases out completely.

So depending on your situation, it may be worth delaying a raise or sale to qualify for those deductions.

Talk to your tax preparer.

In Closing

As noted earlier, your rental business may not feel like *The Holiday*—no dreamy English cottage or Jude Law in sight—but a tax-smart strategy can still give you that feel-good finale.

If only tax deductions were as charming as Jude Law, we'd all file early.

CHAPTER SEVEN

The Strategic Giver

How to Donate Like a Philanthropist and Save Like a Pro

Mastering Donor-Advised Funds, "Bunching" Strategies, and the New OBBBA Charitable Rules

The One Big Beautiful Bill Act was signed into law in July 2025. However, several of its most complex charitable-giving provisions are effective starting in tax year 2026 and require additional IRS regulations, forms, and calculation guidance.

The Tax Fundamentals (Before You Give)

TIP 108
Itemize to Deduct (Still the Gatekeeper)

First and foremost, you need to itemize your deductions on Schedule A to claim a federal charitable deduction. If your total itemized deductions, including state and local taxes, mortgage interest, and charitable gifts, do not exceed the standard deduction for your filing status, your charitable contributions provide no immediate federal tax benefit.

TIP 109

Use the "Bunching" Strategy

Because the standard deduction is high, many taxpayers benefit from bunching multiple years of charitable gifts into a single tax year. So plan your charitable giving accordingly.

In the bunching year, your deductions could exceed the standard deduction, allowing you to itemize.

In off years, you can revert to the standard deduction, maximizing tax efficiency over time.

TIP 110

Verify the Charity's Status

Only contributions to IRS-qualified 501(c)(3) organizations are deductible. Gifts to individuals, political organizations, or nonqualified foreign charities do not qualify.

Always verify eligibility using the IRS Tax Exempt Organization Search on the IRS's website.

A charity's mission statement or website is not enough. For tax purposes, deductibility hinges on whether the IRS recognizes the organization as a 501(c)(3). So be sure to verify.

TIP 111

Keep Proper Documentation

Like all things tax-related, documentation is key. For any single contribution of $250 or more, you must obtain written acknowledgment from the charity confirming the donation amount and whether goods or services were received.

Without this documentation, the IRS may disallow the deduction.

Let's get more specific now.

TIP 112

Cash Donations: The Simplest and Cleanest Charitable Deduction

Cash gifts are the gold standard of charitable giving from a tax perspective. They are easy to document, are easy to value, and carry the lowest audit risk.

What qualifies as "cash"?

- Checks
- Credit cards
- Electronic transfers (ACH, Venmo, PayPal if made to a qualified charity)
- Payroll deductions
- Qualified charitable distributions (QCDs) from IRAs (age 70½+)

Regarding tax treatment, cash donations are:

- Deductible at face value
- Subject to annual AGI limits (generally up to 60% of AGI for gifts to public charities)

So when making a cash donation, be sure to get:

- Either a bank record (check, statement, or electronic receipt)
- Or written acknowledgment for any single gift of $250 or more

Why cash is favored:

- No valuation disputes
- No condition requirements
- Immediately usable by the charity
- Straightforward IRS documentation

Bottom line: If simplicity, certainty, and audit safety matter, cash donations are hard to beat (IRC 170).

TIP 113

Clothing and Household Goods: Condition and Valuation Matter

Donations of clothing, furniture, and household goods can be deductible, but only if some IRS rules are met.

The IRS explicitly disallows deductions for poor-condition items:

- Items must be in "good used condition or better."
- Torn, stained, broken, or unusable items are not deductible.

In regard to valuation:

- You may deduct the item's fair market value, not what you originally paid.
- Fair market value generally reflects thrift-store pricing, not retail.
- Overvaluation is a common audit trigger.

Documentation is required:

- You will need a receipt from the charity describing the donated items.

- If total noncash donations exceed $500, you will need to file Form 8283 (Section A).
- If total noncash donations exceed $5,000, a qualified appraisal is required (with limited exceptions).

Common mistake: Using the original purchase price instead of the resale value. The IRS expects realistic, secondhand pricing.

Bottom line: Clothing and household donations can generate deductions, but only when condition, value, and paperwork are handled carefully (IRC 170).

TIP 114

Vehicle Donations: Special Rules, Lower Expectations

Vehicle donations (cars, boats, airplanes) are highly regulated and often misunderstood. The deduction is rarely what donors expect.

If the charity sells the vehicle:

- Your deduction is generally limited to the gross sales proceeds (which are often much lower than you'd expect).
- The charity must provide Form 1098-C.
- Without Form 1098-C, the deduction may be denied.

If the charity keeps and uses the vehicle, you may deduct the fair market value.

The charity must certify:

- Either intended use
- Or material improvement of the vehicle

Big note: Most charities sell donated vehicles quickly, which means the deduction is, again, often far lower than the car's perceived value.

Bottom line: Vehicle donations can still be generous and helpful, but the tax benefit is often modest unless the charity keeps and uses the vehicle (IRC 170(f)(12)).

TIP 115

Deduct Only the Net Gift

If you receive something of value in exchange for your donation (such as gala tickets or auction items), only the amount exceeding fair market value is deductible.

Charities are required to disclose the nondeductible portion.

Be sure to save your invite.

Maximizing the Asset You Donate

TIP 116

Don't Donate "Losers"

If an investment has declined in value, sell it first so you realize the capital loss.

Then donate the cash proceeds. This way you get the tax loss and the charitable deduction.

TIP 117

Donate "Winners" (Appreciated Stock)

Donating long-term appreciated publicly traded stock is one of the most tax-efficient ways to give:

- You deduct the full fair market value.

- You avoid capital gains tax on the appreciation, which could be up to 20% federally, plus any applicable state tax.

TIP 118
Understand the AGI Deduction Limits

Charitable deductions are subject to annual AGI limits:

- Cash gifts to public charities: Up to 60% of AGI
- Long-term capital gain property: Up to 30% of AGI

TIP 119
Carry Forward Excess Gifts

Amounts exceeding annual AGI limits are not lost.

They may be carried forward for up to five future tax years, which is especially useful when making large or bunched contributions.

So keep track.

TIP 120
Use a Qualified Charitable Distribution (QCD)

As we discussed in Tip 27, if you are age 70½ or older, you may donate up to $108,000 per year (2025 number) directly from an IRA to a qualified public charity.

Three positives:

- The donation counts toward your required minimum distributions.
- It is excluded from taxable income.
- You don't need to itemize to get this benefit.

This is exactly why QCDs still remain one of the most powerful charitable tools for retirees.

TIP 121

The Power of Donor-Advised Funds (DAFs)

A donor-advised fund allows you to separate the tax decision from the charitable decision, and that flexibility is what makes DAFs so effective.

When you contribute cash or appreciated assets to a DAF, you receive the full charitable deduction in the year of the contribution, even if the funds are not distributed to charities until years later.

This is what makes a DAF especially attractive in those high-income years when maximizing your deductions matters most.

Once assets are inside the DAF, they can be invested and *grow tax-free*, allowing earnings to compound over time. That growth ultimately increases the amount available for future charitable grants, amplifying the long-term impact of your giving.

DAFs are also ideal for bunching strategies. You can make a large contribution in one year to ensure you itemize and capture the deduction; then you can recommend grants gradually over time while taking the standard deduction in later years.

From an administrative standpoint, DAFs dramatically simplify recordkeeping. Rather than tracking receipts from multiple charities, you receive *one acknowledgment from the DAF sponsor*, regardless of how many organizations you support.

Finally, DAFs offer flexibility around *privacy*. Grants can be made anonymously if desired, allowing you to give generously without unwanted attention or solicitation.

Example: Using a DAF to maximize impact and tax efficiency. Samantha has a strong commitment to charitable giving and typically donates about $15,000 per year to a mix of local nonprofits.

In most years, however, her total itemized deductions fall below the standard deduction, so her generosity provides little or no federal tax benefit.

In 2026, Samantha has an unusually high-income year due to a bonus and the sale of appreciated stock. Instead of making her usual annual gifts, she contributes $75,000 of long-term appreciated stock to a DAF.

Here's what happens:

- **Immediate tax deduction.** Samantha receives a charitable deduction for the full fair market value of the stock in the year she funds the DAF, allowing her to itemize and significantly reduce her taxable income in a high-income year.
- **Capital gains avoided.** Because she donated appreciated stock rather than selling it, Samantha avoids paying capital gains tax on the appreciation entirely.
- **Tax-free growth inside the DAF.** The assets inside the DAF are invested and can grow tax-free, increasing the total amount available for future charitable grants.
- **Grants made over time.** Over the next five years, Samantha recommends grants of $15,000 per year from the DAF to her favorite charities, maintaining her normal giving pattern without needing to itemize in those later years.
- **Simplified records.** For tax purposes, Samantha keeps one receipt from the DAF sponsor for the original contribution, rather than tracking acknowledgments from multiple charities each year.
- **Optional privacy.** Samantha chooses to make some grants anonymously, supporting causes she cares about without unwanted solicitations.

- **The result.** Samantha aligns her charitable giving with her cash flow, captures the tax benefit when it matters most, and still supports her charities consistently over time.

A donor-advised fund allows donors to separate the timing of the tax deduction from the timing of the charitable gifts, making it one of the most flexible and effective tools for strategic philanthropy.

Total win!!

TIP 122

Charitable Remainder Trusts (CRTs)

A CRT allows you to turn highly appreciated assets into a *reliable income stream* while supporting a charitable cause.

You contribute assets, such as appreciated securities, real estate, or a closely held business interest, to the trust and, in return, receive income either for your lifetime or for a fixed term of years (up to 20).

One of the CRT's most powerful advantages is its ability to *defer immediate capital gains taxes.*

Because the trust itself is a tax-exempt entity, it can sell the contributed assets without triggering capital gains at the time of sale. That allows the full proceeds to be reinvested inside the trust, potentially producing a larger income stream and a greater ultimate benefit for charity.

You also receive a *partial income tax deduction in the year the trust is funded.* This deduction is calculated using IRS actuarial tables and represents the present value of the portion of the trust assets expected to pass to charity at the end of the trust term.

The size of the deduction depends on factors such as payout rate, term length, and prevailing interest rates, so be sure to get your tax advisor involved.

CRTs can also play an important role in estate planning. Because a charitable remainder trust is *irrevocable*, once assets are transferred into the trust, *you cannot take them back or change your mind later.* That permanence is exactly what gives the strategy its estate-planning power.

By funding an irrevocable CRT, the assets are *removed from your taxable estate at the time of transfer*, even though you may continue to receive income from them for years or for life. This can reduce future estate tax exposure while still allowing you to maintain an income stream and direct a meaningful gift to charity.

This structure adds flexibility to legacy planning, particularly in an environment where estate tax thresholds and rules remain subject to change.

For families with charitable intent, a CRT can help balance income needs today with long-term wealth transfer goals—so be sure to speak to your advisor.

TIP 123

CRAT Vs. CRUT: Two Ways a CRT Can Pay You

Charitable remainder trusts come in two primary forms, and the key difference is *how your income is calculated over time.*

A charitable remainder annuity trust (CRAT) pays you a *fixed dollar amount every year*, regardless of how the trust's investments perform. The payout is set when the trust is created and never changes. This can appeal to donors who value *predictability and stability*, especially if they want a steady income stream they can easily budget around.

The trade-off is that the payment does not adjust for inflation or changes in asset value.

A charitable remainder unitrust (CRUT) pays you a *fixed percentage of the trust's value*, recalculated each year based on the trust's current assets. So if the trust grows, your income can increase; if the value declines, payments may go down.

Because the payout is tied to asset value, a CRUT offers *built-in inflation protection* and the potential for rising income over time, making it a popular choice for donors with a longer time horizon or growth-oriented assets.

Sooooo . . .

- Choose a CRAT if you want certainty and a stable paycheck.
- Choose a CRUT if you want flexibility and income that can grow over time.

But as with everything, speak to your tax advisor about which option is right for you and your family.

OBBBA Charitable Changes (Effective 2026+)

Please note: The OBBBA introduces new structural changes to charitable deductions beginning in 2026, particularly affecting higher-income taxpayers and certain split-interest charitable strategies. While these provisions are enacted law, final IRS regulations and calculation mechanics are still forthcoming.

Potential changes may include:

- New income-based thresholds affecting itemized deductions
- Modified interaction between charitable deductions and overall tax liability

- Expanded rules involving charitable remainder structures and retirement assets

Because implementation guidance is still pending, charitable strategies in this book are based on current, fully operational IRS rules. Readers should revisit charitable plans once final IRS regulations are issued for the applicable tax year.

CHAPTER EIGHT

The Hustle Shield

Self-Employed Tax Strategies to Protect Your Profits and Win Under the OBBBA

20 Smart Tax Tips for the Self-Employed

Running your own business takes grit, caffeine, and a whole lot of belief in yourself. The long hours and late nights are real, but so are the rewards when you get to call the shots.

And while you can't expense hustle, you can make the tax code work for it.

So let's do just that. Let's make sure your hard work pays off—not just in profits, but in tax savings too.

Below are 20 smart, simple tips that will help every self-employed pro, freelancer, and small-business owner keep more of what they earn and enter tax season feeling confident and in control.

Everyday Business Deductions

TIP 124

Deduct Business Meals at 50%

You can deduct 50% of business meal costs as long as they are reasonable, they are directly related to your business, and you or an employee is present.

That includes lunches with clients, working dinners, and meals while traveling for business.

Keep your receipts, and note the purpose and attendees on each one—small records make a big difference in an audit.

TIP 125

Separate Meal Costs from Entertainment

Entertainment costs aren't deductible anymore (maybe blame the Wall Street bros for taking too many clients to strip clubs?), but food and drink purchased during those events can be, as long as they're itemized separately.

So if you treat a client to a baseball game, while you can't deduct the tickets, you can deduct half the cost of the snacks and drinks.

Try to ask vendors for itemized receipts—although the folks carrying pretzels and Cracker Jacks may not have that option readily available. Still, it's the easiest way to protect your deduction.

TIP 126

Deduct Meals for Transportation Workers at 80%

Transportation workers, such as long-haul truckers, can deduct up to 80% of their meal costs if they're subject to federal "hours of service" limits.

These hours of service rules were created to prevent fatigue-related accidents, and they apply to most long-haul truckers and interstate drivers.

Under current guidelines:

- Drivers can *drive up to 11 hours* after *10 consecutive hours off duty.*
- The *maximum "on-duty" window* (including driving and breaks) is *14 hours* in a single day.
- Drivers must take a *30-minute break* after 8 consecutive hours of driving.
- Over the course of a week, you can't exceed *60 hours in 7 days* or *70 hours in 8 days*, depending on your schedule.

For tax purposes, transportation workers who are *subject to these rules* can claim *80%* of their meal costs—or the special per diem rate of approximately $86 per day, whichever is more beneficial to them as a deduction—instead of the usual 50% limit for other business travelers.

This higher deduction recognizes the long, irregular hours many transportation professionals face.

And since I don't know how I previously survived without my Amazon drivers, I'm all for it!

TIP 127

Deduct Business Mileage (Standard Rate)

The simplest way to deduct your vehicle use is by tracking your business miles and multiplying them by the IRS standard mileage rate:

- For 2025, the rate is 70 cents per mile for business use.
- For self-employed professionals with a home office, every business mile starts at your front door.

Use a mileage-tracking app—it will simplify the process. Plus if the IRS ever needs proof, it loves to see logs, not estimates.

TIP 128

Deduct Parking and Tolls Separately

Even if you claim the standard mileage deduction, you can still separately deduct parking fees and tolls paid for business travel.

Again, keep digital or paper receipts in a separate folder—these small expenses can add up fast.

TIP 129

Deduct Business Taxes Without a Cap

There's no $10,000 cap on business-related state and local tax deductions—unlike personal SALT deductions. This includes business property taxes, sales taxes, and license fees.

So track these separately from your personal taxes to make sure you don't leave money on the table.

TIP 130

Deduct All Ordinary and Necessary Expenses

If an expense is both ordinary for your business and necessary to operate, it's deductible.

Think office supplies, software, website costs, and even those annoying professional fees.

A smaller taxable profit means a smaller self-employment tax bill—every deduction counts.

TIP 131

Deduct Business Travel Expenses

When you travel overnight for work, you can deduct airfare, lodging, rental cars, and other reasonable costs.

Meals while traveling are still 50% deductible.

Save your receipts, and document the business purpose of each trip—especially if you mix business with pleasure.

TIP 132

Deduct Employee Safety Costs

You can deduct expenses related to employee safety—such as late-night transportation, security, or protective equipment.

While general commuting costs aren't deductible, safety-related expenses are.

Keep a note or policy explaining the safety reason—it strengthens your deduction.

TIP 133

Deduct a Portion of the Self-Employment Tax

Self-employed workers pay both the employer and employee sides of Social Security and Medicare taxes.

The IRS allows you to deduct half of that amount on your personal return as an adjustment to income.

This doesn't reduce your self-employment tax, but it does lower your taxable income, so don't forget to include it.

Smart Tax Strategies and New Law Benefits

TIP 134

Use the Optional Method for Social Security Credits

If your business income is too low to earn Social Security credits in a given year, the IRS lets you use the optional method to boost your contribution.

Normally, self-employed workers earn one SS "credit" for roughly every $1,730 in net profit (2025 figure), up to four credits per year.

But if you didn't make that much, the optional method allows you to pay self-employment tax on a slightly higher, "deemed" amount so you still earn credits toward retirement and disability benefits.

This can be especially helpful for freelancers, seasonal workers, or anyone starting a new business.

Think of it as buying future Social Security eligibility now at a relatively low cost. Those credits can make a big difference later, so talk to your accountant.

TIP 135

Claim the 20% Qualified Business Income (QBI) Deduction

The QBI deduction—the accountants call it the Section 199A deduction—lets many small-business owners deduct up to 20% of their net business income directly from taxable income.

This deduction applies to pass-through entities—meaning businesses where the income "passes through" to your personal return, like sole proprietorships, partnerships, LLCs, and S corps.

So, for example, if your qualified business income (which basically is your net profit after subtracting normal business expenses) is $100,000, you may be able to deduct $20,000, potentially saving thousands in tax.

However, the deduction phases out for high-income earners or certain "specified service" businesses like law, medicine, and consulting.

So confirm your eligibility with your accountant, but it's worth the ask.

TIP 136
Understand the MAGI Limits for the QBI Deduction

To qualify for the full 20% QBI deduction above, your modified adjusted gross income (MAGI) must fall under about $177,000 (single) or $355,000 (married filing jointly) for 2025.

If you're close to those limits, you can defer income—wait to January to bill clients or accelerate expenses and buy needed supplies before year-end—to stay below the threshold.

Timing matters here, so be strategic. Good year-end planning can preserve a valuable deduction that's worth up to one-fifth of your profits.

TIP 137
Consider Becoming a C Corporation (C Corp)

A C corp pays its own taxes separately from you, the owner, and currently benefits from a flat 21% corporate tax rate.

That's lower than many individual tax brackets, so for businesses planning to reinvest profits rather than take them out, it can be attractive.

Of course it's not that simple. The downside is that you are subject to double taxation as a C corp:

1. The corporation pays tax on its income.
2. You pay tax again if you distribute profits as dividends.

The upside, though, is that C corps can also offer benefits like easier access to investors and more retirement-plan options.

So get some professional advice here before you make the switch.

TIP 138

Pay Yourself a Reasonable Salary (S Corporation Strategy)

If your business operates as an S corporation (S corp), you can pay yourself a reasonable salary for the work you perform and take additional profits as distributions. The salary portion is subject to payroll taxes (Social Security and Medicare), but distributions are not—potentially saving you thousands in self-employment tax.

The IRS, however, requires that your pay be "reasonable," meaning comparable to what you'd earn doing similar work for someone else. Paying yourself too little can trigger penalties or an audit.

Work with your accountant to set your salary—it's part art, part science, and a big part of S corp compliance.

TIP 139

Use the Cash Method of Accounting

Small businesses with under $25 million in gross receipts can use the cash method of accounting, which reports income when it's received and expenses when they're paid.

This is much simpler than the accrual method (my accrual accounting class in college still gives me the chills), which tracks income when earned and expenses when incurred, even if cash hasn't changed hands yet.

The cash method gives you more control over taxable income by allowing you to delay invoicing until after year-end or prepay expenses like insurance before December 31.

This flexibility can smooth out cash flow and reduce taxes in high-income years.

TIP 140

Maximize Section 179 Expensing

Section 179 of the voluminous tax code lets you deduct the full cost of qualifying equipment, software, or vehicles in the year you buy them, up to $1,220,000 for 2025, instead of depreciating over time. Depreciating an expense basically means you can deduct a proportion of the expense each year over a determined number of years.

Section 179 lets you take the full expense this year on those qualifying items. So if you had to buy a new cash register, new production equipment, or even a new car, you can deduct the full cost if it's used more than 50% for your business.

The deduction begins to phase out once total purchases exceed $3,050,000, so very large spenders may need to plan accordingly. And the asset must be placed "in service" before year-end, not just purchased—meaning it must be ready and available for use.

TIP 141

Include Used Property for Bonus Depreciation

Bonus depreciation allows businesses to write off 100% of the cost of qualifying assets—new or used—in the year they're placed in service.

This differs from Section 179 because there's no annual dollar cap, and it can create a loss that carries forward.

This stuff gets wonky, but to qualify, the property must have a recovery period of 20 years or less (like vehicles, machinery, or computers).

Again, talk to your accountant, because the percentage deduction will start decreasing after 2026, so now is a great time to use it.

TIP 142

Consider an Office-in-Home Deduction

If you use a portion of your home *exclusively and regularly for business*, you may qualify for the *home-office deduction*. You can choose the *simplified method* ($5 per square foot, up to 300 square feet) or calculate *actual expenses* (like mortgage interest, utilities, and maintenance) based on the business percentage of your home.

This deduction can also make certain local travel deductible—for example, driving from your home office to meet a client counts as business mileage, as we talked about in Tip 127.

The key requirement is "exclusive use," meaning the space can't double as a guest room or playroom.

While it's highly unlikely an IRS agent will come to your home to check, an agent may ask for photos or a floor plan if you are ever audited.

So just be prepared.

TIP 143

Take Advantage of the De Minimis Safe Harbor (DMSH) Rule

For small business owners, the DMSH rule is one of those hidden gems that saves time, money, and paperwork when used correctly.

The DMSH rule lets you immediately expense small business purchases, instead of having to depreciate them over time.

Items that cost $2,500 or less qualify, which covers most everyday purchases like tablets, printers, or office chairs. This rule simplifies recordkeeping and accelerates deductions, especially for businesses with lots of smaller equipment.

Think of the DMSH as the rule for your smaller everyday stuff and Section 179 for your big business investments.

Both get you faster write-offs, but the DMSH is more about simplicity, while Section 179 is about strategy.

As always, keep copies of invoices showing the per-item cost; the IRS will look for that detail if you're ever audited.

Whew! That's was some meaty stuff. But look, proper tax planning isn't just about saving money—it's about rewarding yourself for the hard work and risk that comes with running your own business.

Use these tips to end the year strong, stay compliant, and set yourself up for a profitable 2025.

You've built—or are building—something amazing.

Now make sure the tax code works for you.

The Self-Employed Health Insurance Deduction

If you're an entrepreneur, freelancer, or small-business owner, the self-employed health insurance deduction is one of the best tax breaks available.

It's an *above-the-line deduction*—and you know by now that means it reduces your taxable income even if you take the standard deduction.

So add up all your medical premiums—things like:

- Medical insurance
- Dental insurance
- Vision insurance
- Qualified long-term care insurance (check the limitations)

The coverage can be for you, your spouse, and your dependents.

Bonus: You can also deduct coverage for a child under age 27 at year-end—even if the child is not your dependent.

You may take this deduction if you have earned income from:

- A sole proprietorship (Schedule C)
- A farming business (Schedule F)
- A partnership if you're a general partner
- An S corporation if you own more than 2%

Basically, if you run a business and pay for your own health insurance, this deduction likely applies to you. Great news!

However, there are two big restrictions every self-employed person needs to know:

TIP 144

You Can't Have Access to an Employer Plan

You're not allowed to take this deduction for any month you were eligible in an employer-subsidized health plan. This includes access through your spouse's job. This rule applies month by month, not all or nothing.

TIP 145

Your Deduction Is Limited to Your Earned Income

Your deduction can't be more than the profit from the business that the insurance is tied to.

So if your business had a loss, no deduction.

If your business had $8,000 of profit, you can't deduct more than $8,000 of premiums.

Finally, if you don't qualify for the self-employed health insurance deduction, you may still be able to deduct medical expenses by itemizing them on Schedule A.

Remember though, you only can deduct the portion of your medical costs that exceeds 7.5% of your AGI. Certain medically necessary home improvements, like ramps, wider doorways, or grab bars, can be included and are fully deductible if they don't increase your home's value.

CHAPTER NINE

The Investor's Edge

Mastering Capital Gains, Crypto, and the Stealth "NIIT" Tax

Strategic Plays for Your Portfolio, Retirement Accounts, and the 2026 "Mandatory Roth" Revolution

If you're making smart trading decisions and your portfolio has been doing well, the last thing you want to do is give that back to Uncle Sam.

So let's walk through some strategic ways to manage the tax hit to your investments portfolios and retirement accounts.

Capital Gains and Investment Sales

TIP 146

Try to Hold Investments Long Term

As a refresher, you will owe capital gains tax on the profit you make when you sell an asset, like a stock, bond, mutual fund, cryptocurrency, or even a piece of artwork.

A simple example: You buy a stock for $100. You sell it for $150. You will owe capital gains tax on the $50 gain only.

Now, there are two different capital gains categories—short term and long term:

Short-Term Capital Gains

- Applied to investments held *one year or less* before being sold.
- *Taxed as ordinary income.* That means your *regular income tax brackets* (which range from *10% to 37%* depending on your total taxable income) are applied to the gain. So if you're in the 24% income tax bracket and you sell a stock you held for six months, that gain is taxed at 24%.

Long-Term Capital Gains

- Applied to investments held more than one year before being sold.
- Taxed at special lower rates. That could be 0%, 15%, or 20%, depending on your total taxable income.

Most of us will fall in the 15% or 20% bracket, but that's way better than the ordinary income rates, especially if you're a high earner.

And while you should never make investment decisions based on taxes alone, if possible, try to hold your investments for one year and a day before you sell.

Holding investments for the long haul isn't just about patience—it's about keeping more of your profit.

Remember: Time in the market often beats timing the market—plus it helps your tax bill too.

TIP 147

Practice Tax-Loss Harvesting

If you did sell an investment for a gain this year, you can reduce your tax bill by selling another investment at a loss.

The IRS lets you offset capital gains with capital losses, and if your losses exceed your gains, you can deduct up to $3,000 against ordinary income. Any leftover loss can be carried forward to future years.

Remember: Just don't repurchase the same stock within 30 days, or the "wash sale rule" will void your deduction. But we'll get to that in a minute.

Okay, we need an example here: Let's say you sold an investment for a *$10,000 gain* and another one for a *$15,000 loss, all* in the same year.

- The $10,000 gain less the $15,000 loss leaves you a net loss of *$5,000.*
- *$3,000* of that loss ($1,500 if married filing separately) can be *offset against ordinary income,* like your salary or business earnings, on line 7 of your Form 1040.
- The *remaining $2,000* loss can be *carried forward* to the next year, where you can use it to offset future gains or again deduct up to $3,000 against ordinary income.

So that it doesn't go away, Uncle Sam just doesn't want you to take it all in once. Just keep track of those capital loss carry-forwards because they don't expire, and they can help reduce your future tax bills year after year.

TIP 148

Manage Your Tax Bracket for Capital Gains

So based on the above, if you are making big sells, it may be worth a call to your advisor or accountant.

Remember, your tax rate on long-term capital gains depends on your overall income, so if your income is projected to be a little lower next year, it may make sense to push the sale off if you can qualify for the lower capital gains rate.

Planning when to sell your investments can help you take advantage of these brackets.

Pro tip: Talk with your advisor before selling big holdings—timing can make a big difference.

TIP 149

Donate Appreciated Assets to Charity

Donating appreciated stock or cryptocurrency directly to a charity lets you give more while paying less in taxes—plus it makes you feel good.

You can deduct the full fair market value of the asset as a charitable contribution if you itemize your deductions, and then simultaneously avoid paying capital gains tax on the appreciation.

That's a win-win for both you and your favorite cause. Again, make sure the asset was held for more than a year to qualify for this benefit.

TIP 150

Follow the Wash Sale Rule (IRC §1091)

If you sell a stock, mutual fund, or ETF at a loss and buy the same—or a "substantially identical"—security within 30 days before or 30 days after the sale, the IRS disallows the loss for current tax purposes. This is known as the wash sale rule under IRC §1091.

The intent is simple: the IRS does not want taxpayers claiming a tax loss while maintaining essentially the same investment position. Selling an investment at a loss and immediately buying it back leaves you economically unchanged, so the deduction is temporarily denied.

What Does "Substantially Identical" Mean?

The tax code does not provide a precise definition, but "substantially identical" generally means you have repurchased the same investment or something so similar that it represents the same ownership exposure.

Clear examples include selling a stock at a loss and repurchasing shares of the same company within the wash-sale window, or selling a mutual fund or ETF and buying back the identical fund with the same ticker.

Other situations can fall into gray areas. These may include different share classes of the same company or switching between funds that track similar indexes. In these cases, there is no bright-line rule, so a conservative approach is usually prudent.

The Loss Isn't Gone Forever

A wash-sale loss is not lost—it is deferred. The disallowed loss is added to the cost basis of the replacement shares, which shifts the tax benefit to the future when you eventually sell that position.

The wash sale rule can also affect your holding period. The holding period of the original investment is "tacked on" to the replacement shares, potentially changing whether your next sale is treated as short-term or long-term.

Big Practical Warning

Wash sales can occur across accounts, including between different taxable accounts and, in some cases, involving IRAs. To cleanly harvest losses, wait at least 31 days before repurchasing—or temporarily buy a similar but not substantially identical investment.

Cryptocurrency and Digital Assets

TIP 151

Use the Crypto Wash Sale Loophole—While It Lasts

Speaking of the wash sale rule, it oddly does not apply to cryptocurrency right now. The IRS treats cryptocurrency as a property, not as a security.

Soooo . . . that means the wash sale rule doesn't apply to crypto—*for now*.

That means you can sell a losing crypto position, take the loss for tax purposes, and immediately buy it back. I know—it sounds crazy.

This loophole may close soon if Congress passes new tax legislation. So use it while it's legal—but be sure to double-check current laws before executing the strategy.

TIP 152

Defer Tax on Mining and Staking

If you earn crypto through mining or staking, that income is usually taxable when you receive it.

However, new legislation may allow you to defer the tax until you sell or use the coins.

That change would make it easier to manage cash flow and avoid paying taxes on unrealized gains.

Remember: Stay updated on IRS guidance—these rules can change quickly.

TIP 153

Take Advantage of the De Minimis Exemption—
If It Passes

Lawmakers are discussing a de minimis rule to make small crypto purchases tax-free. This would allow everyday users to spend crypto for small personal transactions without tracking gains.

If passed, it could simplify taxes for casual crypto users.

So keep good records now so if the rule passes, you'll be ready to benefit.

TIP 154

Try to Hold Crypto for over a Year

Just like stocks, cryptocurrency held for more than one year qualifies for lower long-term capital gains tax rates.

Selling too soon could mean paying more in taxes.

Remember: Patience pays—both financially and tax-wise.

CHAPTER TEN

Retirement and Wealth

Mandatory Roth and Long-Term Savings

Retirement and Estate Planning— Keep Your Hard-Earned Money

TIP 155

Maximize Contributions to Retirement Plans

Every dollar you contribute to your IRA or 401(k) is money working for your future—and not going to the IRS.

For 2025, the limit for IRA contributions is $7,000 (plus an extra $1,000 if you're 50 or older).

Traditional IRA contributions may be tax-deductible depending on your income level, while Roth IRA contributions grow tax-free for life.

Your eligibility to contribute to a Roth depends on your modified adjusted gross income (MAGI), which is basically your total income minus certain deductions.

If you and your spouse are *not* covered by a workplace retirement plan:

- Your traditional IRA contributions are *fully deductible*—no income limits apply.
- You can contribute up to *$7,000* ($8,000 if age 50 or older).

If you *are* covered by a retirement plan at work:

- Your ability to deduct depends on your MAGI:

Filing Status	Full Deduction if MAGI ≤	Partial Deduction Up to	No Deduction if MAGI ≥
Single	$77,000	$77,001–$87,000	$87,000+
Married filing jointly (covered spouse)	$123,000	$123,001–$143,000	$143,000+
Married filing jointly (not covered, but spouse is)	$230,000	$230,001–$240,000	$240,000+

(These 2025 thresholds adjust annually for inflation.)

If your income is too high for a deduction:

- You can still contribute to a traditional IRA, but it becomes a *nondeductible contribution* (you'll need to file Form 8606 to track your basis).
- The growth is tax-deferred, and you'll only pay tax on earnings when you withdraw in retirement.

Regardless of the deductibility, think of your IRA as your future paycheck—the earlier you start, the more tax-free growth you enjoy later.

TIP 156

Contribute to a Roth IRA—If You Can

The maximum contribution to all IRAs (Roth or traditional) is *$7,000* if you're under age 50 or *$8,000* if you're age 50 or older (including the $1,000 "catch-up").

To contribute the *full* amount to a Roth IRA, your modified adjusted gross income must be:

- Under $150,000 for *single filers*
- Under $236,000 for *married filing jointly*

If your MAGI falls in the *phaseout range,* you can contribute a *reduced amount*. Once your MAGI exceeds the upper threshold ($165,000 for singles; $246,000 for joint filers), you *cannot contribute directly* to a Roth.

The contribution deadline typically is the tax-filing deadline for that year (April of the next year), so you can make your 2025 contribution by April 2026 if needed.

TIP 157

Take Advantage of the Backdoor Roth

If your income is too high to contribute directly to a Roth IRA, you can still get there through what's called a "backdoor Roth conversion."

Here's how it works: You make a *nondeductible contribution* to a traditional IRA, then *convert those funds to a Roth IRA* soon after—paying tax only on any earnings that occur before the conversion.

Once inside the Roth, your money grows *tax-free for life*, and qualified withdrawals in retirement are *100% tax-free*.

This strategy is completely legal and often used by high-income earners to build tax-free retirement assets even when they exceed Roth income limits.

To avoid surprise taxes, keep your other IRA balances low or separate—because the IRS applies a *pro-rata rule* that blends all your IRAs when calculating how much of the conversion is taxable.

Definitely speak to your advisor.

TIP 158

Prioritize Roth Accounts for the Young'uns

Young professionals have one of the best opportunities for long-term, tax-free growth through Roth IRAs and Roth 401(k)s.

Contributions are made with after-tax dollars, but withdrawals in retirement are completely tax-free. That means decades of compounding growth with no tax bill at the end. Plus, Roth IRAs don't have required minimum distributions (RMDs) during your lifetime.

Encourage your kids or young adults with earned income to open a Roth early—it's one of the smartest financial moves you can make.

RETIREMENT AND WEALTH

TIP 159

Avoid IRA Early Withdrawal Penalties

Withdrawing money from your IRA before age 59½ usually triggers a 10% early withdrawal penalty plus income tax.

Of course there are exceptions, for example, for first-time home purchases or qualified education expenses.

Knowing the rules helps you avoid unnecessary penalties. So always check with your advisor before tapping retirement savings.

TIP 160

Repay 401(k) Loans When You Leave a Job

If you have a 401(k) loan and leave your job, you typically must repay the balance by your next tax filing deadline.

If you don't, the unpaid balance may be considered a taxable withdrawal and could trigger penalties if you're under 59½.

Find out if it's better to roll the loan into your new employer's plan or an IRA to avoid a tax surprise.

TIP 161

Consider a Roth Conversion in Low-Income Years

A Roth conversion means moving money from a traditional IRA to a Roth IRA.

You'll pay taxes now on the converted amount, but future withdrawals will be tax-free. If your income is temporarily lower this year, that's a great time to make the switch.

Converting in a low-tax year can set you up for decades of tax-free income.

TIP 162
Use IRA Funds for Charitable Giving (Qualified Charitable Distributions)

If you're age 70½ or older, you can make a qualified charitable distribution (QCD) directly from your IRA to a charity.

The amount counts toward your RMD but isn't included in your taxable income.

It's a smart—and easy—way to give back and reduce your tax bill.

Big note: The payment must go directly from your IRA custodian to the charity.

TIP 163
Take Advantage of Higher Estate and Gift Tax Exclusions

The One Big Beautiful Bill Act (OBBBA) raises the estate and gift tax exemptions—currently near $13 million per person.

Using these exemptions lets you pass more wealth tax-free during your lifetime or at death. Gifting now can lock in today's high thresholds before future changes.

Large gifts can reduce your taxable estate—consider strategic transfers before year-end.

The gift and estate tax exclusions are always hot topics during legislative discussions, so take advantage of the exemptions while you can.

The 3.8% Net Investment Income Tax (NIIT), Explained Simply

The NIIT, or that pesky 3.8% surtax, is an extra tax that high-income earners may owe on certain types of investment income.

It's completely separate from your regular income tax or capital gains tax. So think of it as an *add-on* tax that kicks in only if you cross specific income levels.

Who has to pay the 3.8% NIIT?

You only owe this tax if your modified adjusted gross income is above certain thresholds:

Filing Status	MAGI Threshold
Married filing jointly/surviving spouse	$250,000
Single/head of household	$200,000
Married filing separately	$125,000

Unfortunately these thresholds have yet to increase with inflation, so more people get swept into the NIIT every year.

Once you pass the threshold, the 3.8% tax applies to whichever is smaller: your net investment income or the amount of your MAGI that exceeds the threshold.

An example: A single filer has $30,000 of investment income, but her MAGI only exceeds the $200,000 threshold by $10,000.

She pays the 3.8% tax on the $10,000, not the full $30,000.

What kind of income is hit with the 3.8% tax?

NIIT applies to most types of passive investment income, including:

- Interest and dividends
- Capital gains (from stocks, real estate, etc.)
- Rental income (unless you're a real estate professional)
- Royalties and annuities
- Income from passive business activities

NIIT *does not* apply to:

- Wages
- Social Security
- Self-employment income
- IRA or 401(k) distributions
- Pension income
- Municipal bond interest (so this is a big planning tool for the wealthy)

So how do you reduce or avoid NIIT?

You have two main goals: Reduce your MAGI, and lower your taxable investment income.

Here's how.

TIP 164

Lower Your MAGI with Smart Contributions

Putting money into tax-advantaged accounts reduces your MAGI and may keep you below the NIIT line.

Examples:

- Traditional 401(k) or 403(b) contributions
- Health Savings Account (HSA) contributions
- Traditional IRA contributions (if eligible)

TIP 165

Use Roth Accounts Strategically

Roth IRA withdrawals don't count toward MAGI and aren't subject to the NIIT. So consider a Roth conversion now to lower your NIIT exposure later.

In addition, Roth withdrawals in retirement do not affect MAGI levels, so this could be a really strong strategy for high earners.

TIP 166

Use Tax-Loss Harvesting

Selling investments at a loss to offset gains keeps your net investment income lower, potentially keeping you under the NIIT threshold entirely.

TIP 167

Consider Municipal Bonds

As a reminder, interest from municipal bonds is tax-free, so that means it is not included in MAGI or net investment income. This makes muni bonds incredibly powerful for high-income investors hovering near the NIIT line.

The NIIT is basically a "stealth tax" on investment income once you cross certain income levels.

But with smart planning, like managing MAGI, using Roth strategies, harvesting losses, and leveraging muni bonds, you can dramatically reduce or even eliminate the 3.8% surtax.

DO YOU OWE THE 3.8% NET INVESTMENT INCOME TAX (NIIT)?

Question 1: What's Your Filing Status?

Single or head of household → Threshold is **$200,000**
Married filing jointly → Threshold is **$250,000**
Married filing separately → Threshold is **$125,000**

Question 2: Is Your MAGI Above Your Threshold?

NO → You do *not* owe NIIT.
(Stop here.)
YES → *Continue.*

Question 3: Do You Have Any Net Investment Income (NII)?

NII includes:

- Interest
- Dividends
- Capital gains
- Rental income (passive)
- Royalties
- Annuities
- Income from passive businesses

NII does *not* include:

- Wages
- Social Security
- 401(k)/IRA withdrawals
- Self-employment income
- Municipal bond interest

So do you have any net investment income?
NO → You do *not* owe NIIT. (Even if your MAGI is high, no NII = no NIIT.)
(Stop here.)
YES → *Continue to Step 1.*

Step 1: Calculate the Two Numbers the IRS Looks At

The 3.8% NIIT applies to the *smaller* of:

- Your net investment income
  or
- The amount your MAGI exceeds your threshold

Step 2: Apply the Tax

Take the *smaller number* from Step 1 and multiply it by 3.8%. That's your NIIT liability.

Example walkthrough (built into the flow):
Filing status: Single → threshold $200,000
MAGI: **$215,000** → over by $15,000
Net investment income: **$40,000**

NIIT applies to the smaller of:
NII: $40,000
MAGI overage: $15,000
Tax is on **$15,000 × 3.8% = $570**

What Not to Do

TIP 168

Don't Deduct Investment Fees or Tax Prep Costs

The Tax Cuts and Jobs Act (TCJA) eliminated most miscellaneous deductions, including investment and tax prep fees.
  Paying those expenses doesn't lower your taxes anymore.
  The OBBBA legislation keeps his rule beyond 2026.
  Focus on strategies that still work—don't chase old deductions.

TIP 169

Avoid Paying IRA Fees Out of Pocket

Pay IRA maintenance or transfer fees directly from the IRA. As noted above, the investment fees deduction no longer exists.
  So let your IRA handle its own expenses—it's just easier.

TIP 170

Same with Those Management Fees for Private Funds

Management and advisory fees for private funds aren't deductible any more under current law either.

Unless you're operating as a business, the IRS sees them as personal investment expenses.

Again, confirm with your advisor what qualifies as a business expense before claiming deductions.

TIP 171

Don't Miss Rollover Deadlines

If you move money between retirement accounts, you have 60 days to complete an indirect rollover. Miss that window, and the IRS will treat it as a taxable withdrawal with penalties.

Do a direct trustee-to-trustee transfer whenever possible—it's simpler and safer.

TIP 172

And Finally, a Roth Conversion Reminder

Roth conversions, which we talked about in Tip 161 are permanent.

So once you go Roth, you can't go back—so time it wisely and understand your tax bracket.

By making a few smart moves before year-end, you potentially can lower your tax bill and keep more of your hard-earned money. That's what smart investing—and smart tax planning—is all about.

CHAPTER ELEVEN

The Triple Threat

Turning Your Health Savings Account into a Retirement Powerhouse

Mastering the Only Account Where Your Money Avoids Taxes on Contributions, Growth, and Withdrawals

Medical costs are a reality of life, but the tax code offers relief in two distinct ways: The first is an above-the-line deduction for business owners paying premiums. The second is the powerful, long-term savings allowed by the Health Savings Account (HSA). Understanding these tools can turn a major expense into a major tax advantage.

TIP 173

The Power of the Triple Tax Advantage of Health Savings Accounts

The HSA is often called the "triple tax advantage" tool because it is the single most tax-favored account out there. It is the only account where your money avoids taxation on contributions, growth, *and* withdrawals.

What? Yep.

Here's how it works.

To be eligible for an HSA, you must be enrolled in a high-deductible medical health plan (HDHP).

For 2026:

The minimum deductible on your high-deductible plan must be:
- $1,700 (self only)
- $3,400 (family)

Maximum out-of-pocket limit:
- $8,500 (self only)
- $17,000 (family)

If your plan doesn't meet these IRS definitions, it's not HSA-eligible, even if your insurance company calls it "high deductible."

Also, you can't be someone else's dependent or enrolled in Medicare.

Once you qualify, opening an HSA is surprisingly easy. You don't need a financial advisor, accountant, or even your employer to do it. You do need to make sure you're eligible.

You can open an HSA through:

- A bank or credit union
- An HSA-specialty provider
- A brokerage firm offering investment HSAs
- Your employer's chosen HSA administrator (if they have one)

Once you open your HSA, you benefit in three different ways—the *triple* tax advantage:

1. **Tax-free contributions.** Contributions are fully tax-deductible from your federal income taxes, even if you don't itemize. And much like contributing to your 401(k) plan at work, that will lower your adjusted gross income, which in turn lowers your tax bill.
2. **Tax-free growth.** Depending on the plan options, the money can be invested, and any interest, capital gains, or dividends earned grow tax-free. And unlike an IRA or 401(k), there are no required minimum distributions. So your money can stay in there as long as you like.
3. **Tax-free withdrawals.** Distributions are tax-free when used for a wide range of qualified medical expenses (deductibles, copayments, vision, dental, and prescriptions).

HSA Contribution Limits for 2026	
Filing Status Individual (self-only)	Limit $4,400
Family coverage	$8,750
Age 55+ catch-up	+$1,000

The HSA is considered a retirement nest egg because the funds roll over year to year and stay with you even if you change jobs or retire.

Age 65 transformation. Once you turn 65, the 20% tax penalty for nonqualified withdrawals is eliminated. At this point, the HSA functions exactly like a traditional IRA: Withdrawals used for nonqualified expenses are taxed as income, but withdrawals for qualified medical expenses remain 100% tax-free.

Long-term strategy. A smart financial strategy is to pay current medical bills out of pocket and save the receipts. The HSA funds are left to grow tax-free. You can reimburse yourself for those old, accumulated medical expenses decades later (in retirement) without paying any tax, provided the expense was incurred *after* the HSA was established.

Now really quick, let's talk through what happens when an HSA owner dies:

1. **Surviving spouse is the beneficiary—most favorable outcome.** If the deceased HSA owner's surviving spouse is the named beneficiary, the HSA automatically transfers to the spouse, and it is treated as the surviving spouse's own HSA as of the date of death.

   That means no tax bill and the money remains in the HSA. Then the surviving spouse assumes all the original tax benefits and can continue to use the HSA funds tax-free for their own qualified medical expenses and can designate a new beneficiary.

2. **Non-spouse is the beneficiary—least favorable outcome.** If the beneficiary is anyone other than the surviving spouse (e.g., a child, friend, or domestic partner), the account immediately ceases to be an HSA upon the owner's death. So then the fair market value (FMV) of the account at the date of death becomes taxable income to the non-spouse beneficiary in the year of the owner's death.

   The beneficiary can reduce the taxable amount by using any HSA funds to pay for the deceased owner's qualified medical expenses that were incurred provided those expenses are paid within one year after the date of death.

CHAPTER TWELVE

The Fast Lane

Mastering the Road Rules for Maximum Auto Deductions

How to Turn Your Business Vehicle into a High-Performance Tax Shield

In *Ferris Bueller's Day Off*, everyone worshiped that rare 1961 Ferrari California Spyder.

But historic cars aren't just to be admired. Under the tax code, they actually can drive your tax bill down.

Whether you're self-employed, running a side gig, ridesharing, consulting, or visiting clients, the IRS actually *wants* you to deduct legitimate auto expenses. Just follow the rules.

You don't need a parade float to ride on or a plan to run the odometer backward like they did in that infamous movie either. Just documentation, clarity, and strategy. So let's take this next section out for a spin.

TIP 174

Start with Total Miles—No Fake Reverse-Odometer Tricks

Remember Ferris trying to back the Ferrari down the mileage ramp to turn back the odometer? Funny scene, but IRC 274(d) requires actual odometer readings, not wishful thinking.

So do yourself, and your CPA, a favor. Take a photo of the odometer on January 1 and then again December 31. This makes it easier to figure out the percentage of those miles that were actually used for your Schedule C.

TIP 175

Log Business Trips Like You're Planning the Perfect Skip Day

The IRS wants details, so use a spreadsheet or an app to keep track of everything, including date, destination, miles, and business purpose—all required by IRC 274(d).

It's super important to separate personal miles from business miles and document it all. If it's not written down, the IRS assumes it never happened.

TIP 176

Standard Mileage Vs. Actual Expenses— You Get to Choose

So how do you calculate your deductible mileage?

Sometimes the standard mileage rate, allowed under IRC §274(i), is easy and efficient.

You basically apply the IRS's standard mileage rate to the miles you've driven, using the rates:

Purpose of Travel	2025 Standard Mileage Rate
Business use (self-employed/contractors)	70 cents per mile
Medical purposes	21 cents per mile
Moving (active-duty military only)	21 cents per mile
Charitable organizations	14 cents per mile

Other years, the *actual expense method* under IRC162(a), especially with repairs, gas, insurance, and maintenance, may deliver the bigger deduction. You just need to calculate everything—things like gas, oil, insurance, registration, repairs, etc., are all deductible based on business-use percentage, according to the IRS.

Big note: If you use the actual expense method in the first year a vehicle is placed in business service, you generally cannot switch to the standard mileage rate in a later year.

TIP 177

Checklist to Pick a Method

Maybe this helps:

Choose the standard mileage rate (SMR) if:

- You want simplicity—one IRS-approved per-mile number, no math gymnastics.
- You don't reliably keep receipts, invoices, or gas/repair records.
- Your car gets good gas mileage and has low annual operating costs.
- You put a lot of business miles on the vehicle.
- You want flexibility to switch to the actual expense method in future years.
- You're leasing the vehicle and prefer predictable deductions.
- You're in year one of business use and want to preserve future options.

- You already track miles under IRC §274(d) using an app or log.

Choose the actual expense method if:

- Your car is expensive to operate—i.e., repairs, insurance, tires, fuel, etc.
- You drive fewer business miles but spend a lot keeping the vehicle running.
- You want to deduct depreciation, interest, or high registration fees.
- You bought a newer or pricier business vehicle this year.
- You already save and organize receipts (or have software doing it).
- You're comfortable calculating your business-use percentage under IRC §162(a).
- You're okay being locked in if you start the actual expense method in year one.

Regardless of the method you choose, keep meticulous records and hold on to them for at least three years after filing your return.

TIP 178

Luxury Car Depreciation Has Limits— Apologies to the Ferrari Owners

Congress must have seen both *Goodfellas* and *Ferris Bueller* and said, "No unlimited write-offs for fancy cars."

Enter IRC 280F, which caps depreciation for passenger vehicles under 6,000 pounds.

Translation: Beautiful red convertibles make terrible tax strategies. They may be great for social media, less so for deductions.

TIP 179
Want a Big Deduction? Think SUV, Not Ferrari

The Ferrari was light, delicate, emotion-inducing—the complete opposite of a powerhouse tax deduction.

For business owners, purchasing a heavy vehicle, specifically one with a Gross Vehicle Weight Rating (GVWR) that exceeds 6,000 pounds, could prove to be a pretty key tax strategy.

So other than those heavy-duty pickup trucks, think SUVs like the Ford Expedition, Cadillac Escalade, or Chevy Tahoe.

These heavier vehicles are often fully deductible in the first year of ownership using Section 179 expensing, up to the maximum deduction annual limit (which is $1.22 million for 2025). And the vehicle must be used more than 50% for business.

These big cars may not be glamorous, but they're great for expensing—and therefore your tax return.

Sometimes the practical car can be the hero too.

TIP 180
A Home Office Turns Every Trip into a Business Trip

The distinction between deductible business travel and nondeductible commuting is a critical area for any business owner.

Okay, so generally, the trip from your home to any fixed workplace, aka your regular commute, is considered a personal expense and cannot be written off.

However, establishing a qualifying home office, as we discussed in Tip 142, fundamentally changes this rule by legally redefining where your business activities start.

As we mentioned, under IRC 280A, your home office must meet two strict tests: It must be used *exclusively* and *regularly* as your principal place of business.

Once your home qualifies as your principal place of business, you eliminate that nondeductible commute entirely that we discussed in Tip 174.

Suddenly, mileage driven from your home to client meetings, vendor locations, coworking spaces, networking events, or even the bank or post office is converted into deductible business travel.

This allows you to claim the mileage deduction for every business trip starting and ending at your front door, significantly boosting your overall auto deduction.

TIP 181

Rideshare Drivers Are Businesses—Even if It's a Side Gig

If Ferris had Uber, he'd be unstoppable, and so is your deduction potential.

Under IRC 162(a), Uber and Lyft mileage is deductible because you're self-employed. And IRC 1402 reminds you that self-employment tax applies, so deductions help soften the impact.

But I can't say it enough—track every passenger mile.

TIP 182

Yes, Even Cash Tips Count

The IRS considers all income taxable under IRC 61(a)—that means digital, cash, Venmo, whatever. Report it; track it; deduct related expenses.

Because the only thing worse than denting a Ferrari? An audit for underreported tips.

TIP 183

Advertising Wrap? You've Turned Your Car into a Business Asset

If you are brave enough to drive around with a branded wrap on your car that advertises your business or a third party, Uncle Sam rewards that bravery.

The act of wrapping your car for advertising converts the vehicle into a bona fide business asset for tax purposes. Even better, this conversion allows you to use IRC 162(a) (Trade or Business Expenses), which says you can deduct expenses, whether you use standard business mileage or actual operating costs, to the extent that is permitted on Schedule C.

So that means this strategy allows you to turn nondeductible commuting mileage (home to work) into fully deductible business mileage, as the car is actively working as an advertisement.

Any of the income generated by the wrap allows you to legally claim a deduction for the true business costs of operating your vehicle. So that branded wrap doesn't just turn heads in traffic; it can also unlock significant tax deductions that were previously inaccessible when the vehicle was purely personal.

So be sure to mention to your tax preparer that you're driving around in a mobile advertisement.

TIP 184

Parking and Tolls—The Little Deductions That Add Up

Ferris may not have cared where they parked, but the IRS does.

Garage fees, parking meter fees, and road tolls—if incurred while traveling for business—are separately deductible expenses.

You can claim these costs in addition to the standard mileage rate. This prevents a large portion of your travel costs from being swallowed by the SMR calculation.

As always, save those receipts.

For Nonbusiness Drivers

TIP 185

Charitable Mileage—Doing Good Still Gets 14 Cents per Mile

Driving to attend volunteer meetings, make charitable food deliveries, go to fundraising events, or attend board activities may not pay emotionally, but it can qualify for a tiny tax break.

You can deduct 14 cents per mile that you drive to any of those charitable events. And while that may not seem like much, if you itemize your deductions, every logged mile counts.

So keep a record of dates, destinations, mileage, and the qualifying charitable organization.

TIP 186

Charitable Parking and Tolls—Also Deductible

Same goes for those parking fees and tolls. As a charitable volunteer, you shouldn't be financially penalized for showing up to help, which is why IRC 170(a) allows deductions for unreimbursed out-of-pocket expenses like parking garage fees and bridge tolls.

So take pictures, save statements, and document the purpose.

Big note: If the organization reimburses you, you can't deduct the expense.

TIP 187

Medical Mileage. Sometimes Necessary, Sometimes Deductible

Trips to doctors, specialists, pharmacies, hospitals, or medical testing facilities may qualify as deductible medical transportation under IRC 213(d)(1)(B), but only if you itemize your deductions on Schedule A and your total medical costs exceed 7.5% of your AGI.

The mileage rate changes annually, so verify before filing. Keep a mileage log with appointment dates and destinations.

This deduction especially helps retirees, chronic-care patients, and caregivers who frequently drive others for treatment.

TIP 188

Moving Expenses? Nope.

Before 2018, taxpayers could deduct moving-related transportation, but TCJA put that deduction on hold, and IRC 217(k) continues that suspension through 2025.

The only exception? If you are an active-duty military member relocating under official orders, you can still claim moving expenses.

TIP 189

Standard Mileage Includes Depreciation— Don't Forget This

Every time you use the standard mileage rate, the IRS quietly assumes that a chunk of that rate represents depreciation, meaning your car's tax basis shrinks under IRC 1016.

When you eventually sell or trade in the vehicle, the IRS expects you to subtract that accumulated depreciation before calculating gain.

If the sale price exceeds your adjusted basis, part may be taxable.

Track mileage by year so you're not reconstructing basis during tax season panic.

TIP 190

Personal Property Taxes May Be Deductible— If They Qualify

Not every vehicle registration fee is deductible; only the portion based on the value of the car qualifies as personal property tax under IRC 164(a).

Flat administrative fees? Not deductible.

But even if it qualifies, the deduction is lumped into your state and local tax total deduction, which is $40,000 under the OBBBA.

TIP 191

Buying Vs. Leasing? Run the Numbers

Buying may offer bigger deductions because of the ability to expense stuff (IRC 179) and calculate that bonus depreciation as mentioned in Tip 141, which accelerate write-offs, especially for eligible business vehicles.

Leasing tends to offer simpler, steadier deductions but usually yields smaller annual tax benefits.

The right answer depends on business use, cash flow, and vehicle price and how long you plan to keep the car, so run projections and talk to your accountant before you sign anything.

TIP 192

Employer Reimbursements Mean No Double Dipping

Remember, if your employer reimburses mileage, you can't claim those miles as a personal deduction—the IRS doesn't reward the same expense twice.

When it comes to auto deductions, the IRS isn't trying to trick you; it just wants proof, purpose, and a little structure. Track your miles, choose the method that saves you the most, keep your receipts, and be honest about when your car is working and when it's joyriding.

As Ferris Bueller reminds us, "Life moves pretty fast. If you don't stop and look around once in a while, you could miss it."

CHAPTER THIRTEEN

Wait . . . You Tried to Deduct What?

Debunking the Wildest Tax Myths in the Book

From "Business Dogs" to "Networking Weddings"—Separating Fact from Financial Fiction

This chapter is for anyone who's tried to deduct a vacation, a wedding, a dog, . . . or their entire personality.

Taxes bring out people's creativity in the most surprising ways.

I have heard some pretty amazing claims from smart, successful taxpayers:

- "My dog is basically my child."
- "I networked at my wedding."
- "That vacation was technically a business trip."

And while I love the hustle, the IRS doesn't grade on effort—it grades on rules. This chapter is a reality check (with a little humor) on the deductions people swear are legitimate, but that don't hold up under IRS scrutiny.

Consider this your "myth-busting" guide to the write-offs that can trigger costly mistakes, unwanted audit attention, or penalties—and how to stay on the right side of the tax code while still taking every legal deduction you actually deserve.

TIP 193

"My Dog Is My Security System— So He's a Business Expense."

Nice try, but unless your dog is trained and certified as a guard animal for a business property, he's not deductible. The IRS doesn't care how loudly he barks at the mailman or how much he hates your ex.

Food, vet bills, and pet toys are personal expenses, even if Fido keeps your home "safe."

There *are* exceptions for actual working animals (think K-9s or livestock guardians). But for most of us, your golden retriever is still just a dependent in spirit, not on your tax return.

TIP 194

"I Can Deduct My Wedding Because I Networked There."

That's impressive, but no. Your wedding, no matter how many business cards you handed out between the vows and the champagne toast, is a personal event.

The same goes for any other personal celebration. The IRS is clear here. You cannot call that "business marketing" and deduct its cost.

The only possible loophole is if you legitimately used part of it for your business—say, you filmed the entire thing as content for your wedding-planning company or YouTube channel.

But unless your big day came with a 1099, it's love, not a line item.

TIP 195

"My Vacation Was a Business Trip Because I Talked About Work."

Chatting about your start-up over sangria in Cabo doesn't make your flight deductible.

To count as business travel, your *primary purpose* for the trip must be business, not leisure.

That means scheduled meetings, documented agendas, and receipts tied to work.

If you decide to tack on a few vacation days, you can only deduct the business portion, not the beach time.

TIP 196

"I Bought Clothes for Work, So Therefore I Can Write Them Off."

Trust me, I wish.

But unless your job requires specific uniforms that *cannot* double as streetwear, your shopping spree doesn't qualify.

The IRS rule is simple: If the clothing is adaptable to everyday wear, it's personal. That includes blazers, dresses, and even that "work-only" pair of Louboutins.

The one exception? Branded or protective clothing (*think* scrubs, safety gear, or logoed attire).

Sadly, looking fabulous is not tax-deductible—or we'd all be rich.

TIP 197

"I Can Write Off My Kids Because They Help Me on TikTok."

While I do love the idea, the IRS does not.

Unless your child actually works for your business and you issue your child a W-2 or 1099, the IRS says you cannot deduct your kid as a business employee.

Now granted, family members can legitimately be paid for *real* work. Things like modeling, clerical tasks, or even social media content do count, but their work must be documented like any other employee's work.

That means keeping track of time sheets, payment records, and actual business value.

See Tip 64 for more details on hiring your kids.

TIP 198

"My Boat Is for Client Entertainment."

This one sank years ago (*ba dum bump*).

With the 2017 Tax Cuts and Jobs Act, the IRS largely eliminated deductions for client entertainment (boats, golf, sporting events, and, of course, those "gentlemen's clubs," etc.).

That means boat operating costs are *not* deductible, because your boat is considered an entertainment facility under IRC 274(a)(1)(B). Expenses for entertainment facilities, including depreciation, fuel, maintenance, or dock fees, are nondeductible if used for client entertainment.

Basically, your boat is a toy (albeit an expense one), not a tax break.

You still can deduct 50% of business meals if work is discussed.

And if you *rent out* the boat to someone to use, then that's a legitimate business.

TIP 199

"I Can Deduct My Divorce Attorney. It's My Future Financial Planning!"

The IRS disallows most personal legal expenses, including divorce proceedings, custody disputes, and prenups.

There are a few exceptions: If part of the fee was directly tied to tax advice or investment allocation, that portion may count. But you'll need an itemized billing statement to prove it.

Divorce costs money, unfortunately, but Uncle Sam offers no sympathy for it.

TIP 200

"I Can Write Off My House Because I Host Friends Who Talk About Business."

Entertaining friends and clients at your home doesn't make it a business property.

The IRS looks for regular, exclusive business use, not social gatherings that *might* include business talk over charcuterie.

Hosting your book club or a wine night with networking vibes doesn't qualify either. If it did, everyone would be claiming their living room as "corporate headquarters."

Stick to legitimate home office space here.

TIP 201

"My Gym Membership Is a Health Deduction."

Going to the gym is great for your health, but not your taxes.

The IRS doesn't consider general fitness expenses medical because they're not prescribed treatments.

Even if you work in fitness or "need to look good for your job," that's still personal.

The only way this works is if your doctor formally prescribes exercise for a diagnosed condition and you can prove it.

Otherwise those extra shoulder presses are for you, not the IRS.

TIP 202

"I Can Write Off My Dating App Subscriptions. They're Client Research."

Nice try, but no.

Unless you're literally a dating coach or psychologist or you're running a matchmaking business, your love life is not a tax deduction.

The IRS isn't buying "networking for synergy" as a business purpose.

And no, calling it "market research" won't help either.

Your subscription to Bumble or Hinge is just personal, no matter how many "finance bros" you come across.

TIP 203

"My Tattoo Is Advertising. It Has My Company Logo."

I actually love this idea, but unfortunately Uncle Sam does not.

If you inked your business logo onto your body, we respect your commitment, but you can't take a deduction for it.

The IRS views tattoos as personal expenses, even if you're your own walking billboard.

Same goes for piercings, nail art, and hair color. Personal grooming is never deductible, even if it is fabulous.

TIP 204

"My Pool Is a Medical Expense Because It Reduces My Stress."

This is one of the oldest myths out there.

The IRS only allows pool deductions when they're medically prescribed, say, for physical therapy after an injury, and the expense must exceed 7.5% of your AGI.

Even then, you can only deduct the cost difference between a regular pool and the medically necessary features.

But if your doctor didn't write "install lap pool" on a prescription pad, it's not deductible.

TIP 205

"I Lost Money on Crypto, so I Don't Need to Report It."

Actually, you do.

The IRS treats cryptocurrency as property, meaning gains *and* losses must be reported—even if you traded on an app or never cashed out.

Unreported crypto activity triggers one of the first questions on every 1040: "Did you receive, sell, or exchange any digital asset?"

Answer "no" when you did, and that's kind of perjury territory.

Losses can offset gains and up to $3,000 of other income per year, so you might as well report them and get something back.

TIP 206

"The IRS Doesn't Care About Side Cash."

Oh yes, it does, and yes, the folks there will figure it out.

Know this: Any income you receive is taxable, whether or not you get a W-2, 1099, Venmo payment, or bills from weekend gigs.

The IRS has entire teams and technology devoted to matching income from digital platforms and those third-party processors, like Venmo and Cash App. That's what Form 1099-K, which we talked about in Tip 99, is all about.

Pretending that cash tips or freelance income "doesn't count" is the tax equivalent of holding on to the railing when you step on the scale.

Report it. It's cheaper than getting caught.

TIP 207

"My Vacation Rental Losses Don't Matter Because It's Just a Hobby."

Be careful here.

If the IRS classifies your rental as a hobby, then you lose all your corresponding deductions (see Tip 103).

You must prove a profit motive: Keep records, advertise, adjust pricing, and treat it like a business. Otherwise, those lovely "losses" become nondeductible personal expenses.

The IRS rule of thumb: Show a profit in three of five years, or show clear intent to make one.

The difference between "vacation rental" and "vacation excuse" is paperwork.

TIP 208

"I Don't Need Receipts. The IRS Trusts Me."

That's adorable but unfortunately not true.

The IRS operates on documentation, not trust falls. You don't need a receipt for every coffee, but anything over $75, especially travel, lodging, and gifts, requires proof.

Digital records count, so use apps (I record all my expenses in an app!) or your phone camera to save them.

Auditors love organized taxpayers; they go easier on those with receipts that match the story.

Memory fades; receipts don't.

TIP 209

"If I Owe Less Than $1,000, They Won't Care."

Oh, they care.

The IRS applies penalties and interest no matter how small the balance, and those little amounts compound fast.

Even $200 left unpaid for a year can grow by double digits, thanks to that pesky daily interest. The IRS doesn't forget those small balances because it knows they can grow to be big ones.

Paying in full, even late, closes the account and keeps your compliance record spotless.

TIP 210
"I Don't Have to File if I Didn't Make Much Money."

Maybe, but maybe not.

Even low earners may need to file to claim refundable credits like the Earned Income Credit or Child Tax Credit, which we talked about in Tips 50 and 52.

Plus, filing creates a paper trail that can help with future loans, Social Security benefits, and financial aid. If you had taxes withheld, filing is the *only way* to get that money back. Skipping a return because you think you're "too small to matter" is how refunds disappear forever. The IRS loves unclaimed money—don't donate yours.

TIP 211
"If I Get Audited, I'll Just Say My Accountant Did It."

Nice try, but if you signed the return, it is all you.

Even if a preparer makes a mistake, you're legally responsible for the accuracy of everything on it. A good tax pro can help fix or defend it, but the person can't take the blame.

Always review your return before signing; ignorance is not a defense.

Remember, the IRS won't audit your accountant—it will audit *you*.

TIP 212

"The IRS Won't Notice. I'm Too Small."

This is what everyone says . . . and then they get an audit letter.

The IRS uses algorithms that don't care about fame, fortune, or zip code. They flag math errors, mismatches, and statistical outliers (like an extra-large number of charitable deductions this year).

Even modest returns get auto-checked by systems like DIF (Discriminant Inventory Function).

They don't need to notice *you*, just your numbers.

The best way to stay invisible to the IRS is to be accurate.

CHAPTER FOURTEEN

The Great Extension

Mastering the April Deadline and Staying on Uncle Sam's Good Side

Tax season has a way of turning even the most organized people into professional procrastinators. You tell yourself you're going to stay on top of everything . . . and then out of nowhere you're googling things like "what time does the IRS go to sleep?" and "does it accept Venmo?"

But here's the good news: tax season doesn't have to be stressful—as long as you understand a few simple rules.

So consider this chapter your no-drama guide to the stuff that actually matters: filing deadlines, extensions, what to do if you're missing paperwork, and how to handle it if you owe money and can't pay all at once. Because here's the truth: the IRS doesn't need you to be perfect — but it does need you to respond.

I always say the IRS is like a little kid: it doesn't need a long explanation . . . it just needs to be acknowledged.

In the pages ahead, you'll learn how to file smart, extend properly, avoid common mistakes, and stay in control—so you can get your return done (pat the IRS on the head) . . . and get on with your life.

22 Tax-Smart Tips on Filing, Paying, and Navigating IRS Rules with Confidence

TIP 213

File Electronically. It's Faster, Safer, and Smarter

E-filing isn't just convenient; it's the IRS's preferred method these days.

You typically get an email or text noting your e-filed return was received within 24 hours, and you often see your refund (if you're expecting one) within 21 days.

Paper returns, on the other hand, can take 6 to 12 weeks to process, and of course it's a crap shoot if it even gets there these days.

Electronic filing also drastically reduces errors since math is automatically checked and missing or incorrect info is flagged, like transposed Social Security numbers.

Plus your return is time-stamped with your "file date," so there is no questioning your return is on time and accepted if you are a last-minute filer.

TIP 214

Uncle Sam Needs to Hear from You by April 15

Your tax return is due on April 15 every year, unless it falls on a weekend or a holiday. Then it is due the immediate next day or two afterward.

But if you can't get your paperwork together to file on time, then you must file Form 4868 (Application for Automatic Extension of Time to File). That form will give you an automatic six-month extension to file, which will push your deadline to October 15, unless again it lands on a weekend or holiday.

The ability to extend is super helpful for people waiting on K-1s (the tax forms that report income from a partnership, S corporation, or LLC), brokerage forms, or complicated business statements, because those forms often come beyond the April 15 deadline.

But the key word here is "file" (IRC6081)—file something.

Uncle Sam is expecting to hear from you by midnight on April 15. So if you can't get him your actual return, then absolutely send Form 4868.

TIP 215

Even if You Can't Pay Your Tax Bill—File Anyway!

Many people freeze when they owe money and can't pay it all at once. But take a breath.

First things first. File something, albeit your actual return or an extension.

Because failing to file something can get expensive.

A hefty 5% per month "failure-to-file" penalty kicks in on the amount you owe—IRC 6651(a)(1).

We need a quick example: Let's say you owe $5,000 in federal income tax but you miss the April filing deadline and don't request an extension.

The failure-to-file penalties start immediately. So 5% on your $5,000 outstanding balance = $250.

In the simplest terms, after one month you now owe $5,250—but that doesn't include the interest you also will owe on the outstanding tax balance, which we will get to next.

Moral here: File something!!

TIP 216

Now, Even if You Extend, You Still Have to Pay What You Owe

An extension to file your tax return is *not* an extension to pay your bill.

Let's repeat that: You still have to pay what you owe by April 15, even if you ask for an extension to file your return, or you will owe penalties on the amount due.

Missing that date triggers a failure-to-pay penalty, which currently is 0.5% of your unpaid balance per month.

In our example above, you will owe an additional 0.5% on that $5,000. That's an additional $25.

Your total now after the first month of no filing or paying? $5,275.

So send your best estimate of what you owe by the deadline to minimize the interest and penalties.

TIP 217

If You Owe, Make Your Payment Online

The IRS offers multiple digital payment options that are faster, safer, and easier to track than back in the day when you mailed in a check.

You can pay directly from your bank account through Direct Pay or the Electronic Federal Tax Payment System (EFTPS).

Just make sure your online payment is scheduled by 11:59 p.m. your local time on the due date.

Handling Payment Issues

TIP 218

Set Up an IRS Payment Plan if You Can't Pay in Full

If you can't pay your full tax bill, don't panic. The IRS actually will work with you.

But be proactive. The folks at the IRS will help you if you step up and quickly tell them you need more time.

You can apply online for an installment agreement (payment plan) if you owe less than $50,00 in combined tax, penalties, and interest (IRC 6159).

Approval usually is automatic if you are current on past filings. And you generally can pick the monthly amount you can afford to pay.

You'll still owe interest, but the penalties stop increasing once the plan is in place.

Set this up quickly—don't let that outstanding balance sit there.

TIP 219

Short-Term Payment Extensions— The 180-Day Grace Period

If your tax bill is smaller or you just need a little more time, the IRS offers a short-term payment plan of up to 180 days to pay in full.

There's no setup fee, and you can request it directly online at IRS.gov/payments.

Interest still accrues, but it's often cheaper than using a credit card.

TIP 220

Paying with a Credit Card: Good Idea or Bad One?

It depends.

It can make sense if you are earning rewards or miles or avoiding larger IRS penalties and then pay off the card quickly. Carrying a high-interest balance will quickly defeat the purpose of those reward points.

Also note that the IRS doesn't process credit cards directly. It uses third-party vendors that charge a processing fee (around 1.85%–2%).

So if you use your credit card, treat it as a short-term bridge, not a long-term financing plan.

TIP 221

Track Your Refund (or Payment)

The IRS's "Where's My Refund?" tool updates daily. And generally, it's pretty accurate.

Refunds from e-filed returns usually show up within 21 days if you request direct deposit when filing your return.

On the flip side, refunds from paper returns can take months.

If your refund is taking unusually long, you may have outstanding federal or state debts. Be sure to look into that.

TIP 222

All Refunds Aren't Instant—Even When You E-File

While most refunds arrive within 21 days, additional delays happen when your return hits any of the IRS's review triggers, like identity verification flags, or if you are claiming the Earned Income Tax Credit (EITC), which is subject to an extra review under the Protecting Americans from Tax Hikes (PATH) Act.

The PATH Act of 2015 is a U.S. federal law that has two key components: It provides tax-relief extensions and bolsters tax-fraud/credit-abuse protections.

The latter allows the IRS extra time to verify that you do indeed qualify for the EITC since, as we mentioned, it is often abused.

TIP 223

How to Fix a Mistake: Form 1040-X

If you miss something, you can file Form 1040-X (Amended U.S. Individual Income Tax Return) to fix your error.

You generally have three years from your original filing date to make corrections and claim a refund (IRC 6511).

Again, electronically file these amended returns. It's faster and safer.

Just know that the IRS does go through every 1040-X, so always attach as much explanation and documentation as you can.

TIP 224

Don't Forget to Amend Your State Return Too

If you file an amended federal return (Form 1040-X), you'll likely need to amend your state return as well.

Most states require you to notify them of federal changes and have similar three-year deadlines.

Just wait until the IRS accepts your federal change before filing the state one.

TIP 225

The IRS Does Forgive Penalties—Sometimes

If you normally file and pay on time but slip up once, you may qualify for First-Time Penalty Abatement (FTA), which basically is a one-time get-out-of-jail card.

You can request it by phone if you've been compliant for the prior three years.

The IRS will remove the failure-to-file or failure-to-pay penalties, though interest still applies.

TIP 226

How IRS Interest Really Works— And Why the Penalty Adds Up So Fast

IRS interest accrues daily—not monthly—and keeps compounding until your balance hits zero.

The rate is set quarterly and is indexed to the federal short-term rate plus 3 percentage points (IRC 6621).

Paying early, or even making partial payments, can reduce your balance subject to interest faster than most people realize.

TIP 227

Ignoring IRS Letters Doesn't Make Them Go Away

Nice try though.

If an IRS notice shows up in your mailbox, open it immediately.

Ignoring it will just make the situation worse and could result in a lien, which is a legal claim against your property, or a levy, where it seizes your assets or bank accounts.

The IRS only uses these enforcement actions (IRC 6331) after attempts at communication have been ignored—so don't ignore notices.

Protection and Recordkeeping

TIP 228

Create an IRS Online Account— It's Your Digital Tax Dashboard

Your IRS online account is your secure digital tax dashboard. It allows you to view your balance, payment history, official transcripts (detailed summaries of past returns and account activity), and notices—all in one place.

It's the fastest way to check your standing without spending hours on hold with the IRS.

Here's how to do it:

1. Go to the IRS website: Navigate to "Online Account for Individuals."
2. Click "Sign in or create account."
3. You'll be directed to the identity verification provider, which currently is ID.me.
4. If you don't already have an ID.me account, you can create one. Register with your email, set a password, and then follow instructions to verify your identity (upload a photo ID, take a selfie, etc.).
5. Once your identity is verified, you'll link that profile to your IRS online account. Then again create a username and a password, set security questions, and log in.
6. Then you'll be able to access your account balance, payments, and set up a payment plan, as well as being able to view transcripts, digital notices, etc.
7. Maintain your login, and verify periodically for fraud. And be sure to keep your email address updated in the account for notifications.

TIP 229

Get an IRS Identity Protection PIN (IP PIN) — Especially if You've Ever Been Hacked

An IP PIN is a six-digit number issued by the IRS, used to verify your identity when filing your federal income tax return.

It ensures that no one else can file a return using *your* Social Security number (SSN) or Individual Taxpayer Identification Number (ITIN) without it.

Identity-theft tax fraud is a real and growing risk, so an IP PIN can lock down your tax account so that the IRS rejects any return that is attempted to be filed without your unique PIN.

Here's how to get one:

1. Go to IRS.gov → Get an Identity Protection PIN (IP PIN).
2. If you already have an IRS online account, log in, and under your *Profile* section select the IP PIN program. You again will have to verify your identity (like you did for ID.me or one of the other identity-verification steps).
3. If you can't verify online, you also can apply using Form 15227 (Application for an Identity Protection PIN) if your last-filed AGI falls below $84,000 for individuals or $168,000 for joint filers.
4. Once accepted, the IRS issues your IP PIN each January (if you sign up for continuous enrollment) or will just send you the next tax year's IP PIN.

Just know that the IP PIN is valid *for one calendar year*. Each year you'll need a new one.

TIP 230

Know What "Injured Spouse" Means

"Married filing jointly" is not just a box you check—it creates joint and several liability under IRC 6013(d), meaning the IRS can collect the entire tax bill (or seize the entire refund) from either spouse, even if only one spouse caused the issue.

That's why *injured spouse relief* and *innocent spouse relief* (see the next tip) exist, though they serve totally different purposes.

Okay, injured spouse relief first.

When your spouse has his own separate debt, and the federal government is seizing your joint refund to pay it, you are an injured spouse.

Examples of debts that trigger refund seizure:

- Past-due child support

- Federal student loans in default
- State income tax debt
- Federal agency debts (like unemployment overpayments, etc.)

If your spouse has any of these and the IRS is coming after your refund, use Form 8379—Injured Spouse Allocation.

That form tells the IRS that you are "injured" here and to calculate your share of the refund and return it to you, instead of applying it to your spouse's debt.

You can file the form with your tax return, or even after the IRS offsets your refund. It typically takes 8–14 weeks to process.

You must have earned income, withholding, estimated payments, or refundable credits of your own.

Big note: This does not change your filing status; you still file jointly using IRC 6402.

We need an example: You and your spouse are owed a $2,800 refund. Your spouse owes $5,000 in overdue child support. Without Form 8379, the IRS keeps the whole refund. With it, you may recover the portion attributable to your wages and withholding.

So file the form.

TIP 231

Same with "Innocent Spouse"

If you signed a joint return not knowing your spouse:

- Hid income
- Claimed bogus deductions
- Committed fraud
- Underpaid tax

and the IRS wants you to pay for all that, you are an innocent spouse.

You must file Form 8857—Request for Innocent Spouse Relief.

This form separates your responsibility from your spouse's, which could then relieve you of the tax, penalties, and interest you shouldn't incur.

There are three possible forms of relief under IRC 6015:

- **Innocent spouse relief.** You didn't know about the understatement.
- **Separation of liability.** You're divorced, separated, or living apart.
- **Equitable relief.** Even if you technically knew, forcing you to pay would be unfair (often used in cases of abuse or financial control).

You must file Form 8857 within two years of the IRS first attempting to collect the debt.

Another quick example: Your spouse ran a cash-based business and didn't report income. You had no access to bank accounts and only signed the return because he told you to.

Years later, the IRS wants $22,000. What?? Form 8857 can remove your liability.

So talk to your accountant about this if you feel you qualify.

TIP 232

And My Quick Public Service Announcement

- Don't sign a joint return you haven't reviewed—make sure you understand the wage statements, 1099s, and business records.
- Keep track of your own withholding and estimated payments. This will help with an injured spouse claim.
- Keep copies of every tax return and transcript. An IRS online account makes this easier because it should all be there.

- If you're divorcing, make sure the tax liability responsibilities are in your divorce settlement. The IRS doesn't actually have to agree with it, but it helps your case.
- If you believe you have been subjected to financial abuse, consult an attorney before filing Form 8857.

TIP 233

Keep Your Tax Records—But Not Forever

The IRS recommends keeping most tax documents for at least three years from the date you filed—this is the standard statute of limitations for audit (IRC 6501).

Keep them seven years if you claimed a loss from worthless securities or bad debt.

Employment tax records must be kept for four years after the due date or payment date (IRC 6001).

After that, just shred securely. You don't need the clutter.

TIP 234

Celebrate Responsibly—And Then Make a Note to Start Earlier Next Year

Once you've filed, paid, and saved your confirmations, take a moment to actually exhale.

Review what worked—and what didn't—so next year's process is smoother.

And don't wait until April 14th to start the process next year. Set a note in your calendar as early as February 1st to get going next year.

And if you extended your return this year, remember—the summer flies by, and it will be October before you know it.

CHAPTER FIFTEEN

The Goodfellas Guide to the IRS

Surviving an Audit Without Losing Your Cool

In the movie *Goodfellas*, Henry Hill famously says, "As far back as I can remember, I always wanted to be a gangster."

Nobody has ever said that about being audited.

But unlike Tommy, Jimmy, and Henry, you don't have to panic, disappear, or start digging shallow holes in the middle of the night.

Most audits are routine, boring, and totally survivable—that is, if you know the rules.

Let's break it down, mob-movie style.

How to Dodge the Top 10 Red Flags and Navigate a Sit-Down with the Tax Man

TIP 235

Reporting Round Numbers (aka "The $500 Rule")

If every number on your return ends in 0 or 50, it looks like you guessed.

The IRS's data systems flag "suspiciously tidy math" because real life is messy—expenses are $482, not $500.

Always use actual amounts from receipts, not estimates. Consistent rounding may seem harmless and easy, but it screams "not true."

Accurate numbers appear normal; round ones stand out like neon lights.

TIP 236

Large Deductions Compared with Your Income

When your deductions are wildly out of proportion to your income, say, $90,000 in expenses on $100,000 in revenue, it raises eyebrows. The IRS compares your ratios with industry norms as well as your previous returns.

If your write-offs and deductions look unrealistic, you might be asked to prove them. Legitimate high deductions are fine; just make sure you can back them up.

TIP 237

Unreported 1099 Income

If you get a Form 1099 from work you've done or a transaction you made, report it, because the IRS has a matching copy.

The IRS's computers automatically will compare your return with the data they have, which includes all those 1099s. If the numbers don't match, the IRS will raise that proverbial red flag and send you a CP2000 notice.

A CP2000 notice is a letter from the IRS that indicates the difference between what you reported and what it thinks you should have reported, because it gets *all* the forms, from third parties, like your employer or brokerage firm.

So just know: If you have a form, the IRS has it too.

TIP 238

Claiming 100% Business Use of a Vehicle

Unless you drive a van full of plumbing tools or a delivery truck, 100% business use of your car looks sketchy.

You can deduct your business percentage, but claiming total business use of your Mercedes C-class, which also takes you to the gym and food store, is a hard sell.

So keep a mileage log, digital tracker, or written calendar to prove your case.

The IRS can smell "creative commuting" a mile away.

TIP 239

Excessive Meal and Entertainment Deductions

As you know by now, business meals are 50% deductible, but entertainment expenses are largely disallowed since 2017.

Yet people still try to get creative and write off concerts, golf trips, and wine tastings under "client development."

But the IRS is on to you.

So keep meal receipts, note who attended, and jot a quick "business purpose" so you have some detailed proof.

TIP 240

Home Office Abuse

The home office deduction is great when it's legitimate.

The space must be used "regularly and exclusively" for business.

Using your dining room table or having a desk in the playroom doesn't qualify. The IRS loves this audit target because so many taxpayers stretch the definition.

If you really have a dedicated workspace, take the deduction confidently, but just be ready to prove it.

TIP 241

Cash-Heavy Businesses

Restaurants, salons, landscapers, and other cash-based businesses are prime audit territory.

The IRS knows how easy it is to underreport income when transactions aren't digital.

If you're in one of these industries, keep meticulous daily logs, deposit slips, and point-of-sale reports. Inconsistent deposits or round-number cash totals are red flags.

The more transparent your paper trail, the safer you are.

TIP 242

Claiming the Earned Income Tax Credit (EITC) Incorrectly

The EITC is a valuable credit for working families, but it's also one of the most misclaimed.

As a reminder, the EITC is a valuable, refundable federal tax credit specifically for low-income to moderate-income working individuals and families. The amount of the credit depends on your income and filing status and whether you have a qualifying child, with the largest benefits going to working families with children.

For 2024 (which you will file in 2025), the maximum adjusted gross income is $66,819 with a maximum credit of $7,830 for three or more qualifying kids.

The credit helps reduce the amount of tax owed, plus it is refundable, which means you could get a refund of the remaining credit even if you don't owe any tax.

The IRS routinely audits returns claiming it because eligibility rules are strict, especially around income limits, filing status, and dependent definitions.

A single wrong box can trigger a review. If you qualify, good for you—just make sure your paperwork supports it.

The IRS understandably doesn't play around with refundable credits because it pays out cash.

TIP 243

Amending Returns Every Year

Amended returns aren't red flags, but if you file them every year, the IRS starts to wonder.

You're either sloppy or trying to be sneaky.

A one-time correction is fine; a pattern of "Oops, found another deduction!" invites closer inspection.

If you truly discover errors or missed credits, amend confidently; just keep the documentation, and don't make it an annual tradition.

Precision beats revision.

TIP 244

"Hobby" Businesses with Years of Losses

This one's classic, and we talked about this in Tip 103.

The so-called business that never makes money but generates beautiful deductions is a screaming red flag.

The IRS uses Section 183 (the hobby loss rule) to reclassify those "business ventures" as hobbies if there's no profit motive. That means you lose all your deductions.

So if it truly is a business, albeit a losing one, show legitimate effort: Do some marketing, create separate accounts, write a business plan, and show an attempt to turn a profit.

The IRS will respect a business with intent, but if you're trying to get a tax write-off for your passion project, forget it.

Remember, in the tax world, "boring" is beautiful.

Clean numbers, consistent records, and reasonable deductions keep you invisible—a good thing because you do not want the IRS's attention.

What to Do if You Get Audited

TIP 245

Don't Panic—An Audit Isn't an Indictment

Most audits start because a computer flagged something—not because an agent is outside your house in a Crown Vic eating a sandwich.

The IRS sends thousands of automated correspondence audits (think CP-2000 notices) triggered by math errors, missing 1099s, or mismatched W-2s.

But ignoring that correspondence is the *Goodfellas'* version of walking into the Copacabana uninvited—bad move.

Stay calm, read the notice fully, and remember—the fastest way for an audit to spiral is to ignore it and hope it magically goes away.

TIP 246
Know What Kind of Audit You're Dealing With

Every audit has its own personality, much like the *Goodfellas* crew.

A correspondence audit is the polite bartender asking you to pay your tab—send documents and move on.

An office audit means the IRS wants a sit-down, and you bring your documentation in briefcases, not garbage bags.

A field audit? That's the scene where you know the music is about to change, so call in the backup. It's time to hire representation and tighten your recordkeeping. *Note:* IRC 7605(a) says the IRS chooses the time and place of the examination.

Understanding the type of audit helps you react correctly instead of overreacting dramatically.

TIP 247
Respond Before the Deadline—Or Fuggedaboutit

IRS deadlines are not suggestions. They're more like Jimmy Conway's requests—you don't ignore them.

IRS notices usually give you 30 days to respond.

Missing that deadline can trigger penalties—IRC 6651(a)(1)—or a legally binding Notice of Deficiency.

So even if you're waiting for documents, just let the IRS know. Acknowledgment buys goodwill and time.

The IRS would rather you communicate than disappear like Morrie after the wig commercial.

TIP 248
Bring Receipts—Literally

In *Goodfellas*, the smartest guys kept no records.

In the tax world, that'll get you "whacked" financially.

The IRS prioritizes documentation over stories, memories, or "Well, my accountant said . . . " If you can't substantiate it, the deduction may be denied—no hard feelings, just rules.

Things to bring include:

- Receipts
- Invoices
- Bank statements
- Mileage logs
- Canceled checks

Bring it all!!!

Organized paperwork also signals you're credible and cooperative and not hiding a trunk full of unreported income.

TIP 249

Get a Professional—Your Consigliere

You wouldn't walk into a mob sit-down without a trusted advisor—well, same applies here. CPAs, EAs (enrolled agents), and tax attorneys know procedure, terminology, and the human psychology inside the IRS.

They also act as a buffer so you don't nervously overshare, contradict yourself, or sound guilty when you're not.

Legal representation can request transcripts, slow things down, negotiate, and push back when necessary.

The folks at the IRS are far more polite when they know someone is watching the process.

TIP 250

Don't Volunteer Extra Information

Henry Hill's downfall was talking too much. Don't be Henry.

Answer what the IRS asks—truthfully, clearly, directly—and then stop talking.

Volunteering extra details, explanations, or unrelated financial history can accidentally expand the audit.

If they want more, they'll ask, and your representative can navigate it strategically. But IRC 7602(a) says that the IRS can only request relevant information

TIP 251

Get Everything in Writing—No Backroom Deals

A handshake may have worked at the Copacabana, but not with federal agencies. Written records protect you if something gets miscommunicated, misunderstood, or misplaced.

Summarize phone calls in follow-up concise emails: "As discussed . . ."

Save letters, notices, fax confirmations, and email chains as if they were evidence in a courtroom drama. If your case ever escalates, your documentation becomes your alibi.

TIP 252

You Can Appeal. Don't Let One Agent Be Judge and Jury

IRS auditors are human. They make mistakes, misinterpret documents, or apply rules inconsistently.

The Appeals Office exists specifically to provide a fresh set of eyes and resolve disputes without Tax Court.

Many taxpayers win or settle more favorably here because Appeals prefers compromise over confrontation.

And if you need to go to Tax Court, remember—you don't need representation to file the petition. You still have leverage—use it.

TIP 253
Fix Whatever Triggered the Audit

Audits are like warning shots—ignore them and you may see more.

So take the IRS's suggestions seriously. Update your bookkeeping systems, adjust your withholdings, track your business expenses properly, and start using accounting software instead of that dang shoebox.

The IRS absolutely notices repeat offenders. Showing improvement helps if you ever seek penalty relief under reasonable cause.

Think of it like Henry entering witness protection—new habits, clean slate, new life.

TIP 254
Celebrate the Win—Even if You Owe Money

An audit resolved, even with a balance due, is still a victory.

You survived, learned, organized your financial life, and avoided deeper consequences.

Many taxpayers walk away more confident and disciplined—which saves far more money over time.

So congratulate yourself. Peace of mind is the real refund here.

Like Henry Hill says near the end of *Goodfellas*: "In the end, it was easier than I thought. I just had to follow the rules."

That's an audit in a nutshell. So stay calm, stay organized, answer what's asked, and get help when needed, and life goes on.

No hidden cash or witness protection—just paperwork, deadlines, and professionalism.

And if the IRS ever comes calling again, you won't panic because now you know how to get it done.

Conclusion

If there's one thing I hope you take away from this book, it's this: You don't need to know everything about the tax code to make good decisions, but you do need to know enough to ask the right questions.

The rules we've walked through in these chapters will continue to evolve. Congress will revise them. The IRS will issue new guidance. States will add their own twists. That's the nature of tax law (and why accountants have jobs), and it's why awareness and planning matter far more than memorization.

What doesn't change is the value of being informed.

When you understand the big picture—where opportunities exist, where limitations apply, and where mistakes tend to happen—you're far better positioned to protect your money, make confident decisions, and avoid costly surprises.

This book is meant to give you that foundation.

A Final (and Important) Reminder

Nothing in this book is intended to replace personalized advice.

Your tax situation is unique. Your income, assets, family circumstances, and state of residence all matter. And tax laws are constantly changing.

Before acting on anything you've read here, always check with your CPA, tax preparer, financial advisor, or another qualified tax professional who understands your full financial picture.

Good planning is collaborative—and the best outcomes come from informed conversations with the right professionals.

Staying Current

Because tax rules never stand still, you can find ongoing updates and commentary at:

- tracybyrneswealth.com
- irs.gov

You can use this book as your guidepost and stay current as the rules evolve.

One Last Thought

Taxes don't have to be scary, and they don't have to control your decisions.

With the right information, the right questions, and the right support, they become just another part of a thoughtful financial plan—not a source of stress.

I also hope this book felt a little approachable—dare I say maybe even a little fun—and not nearly as painful as you expected. Taxes are serious, but learning about them doesn't have to be miserable. A bit of clarity (and maybe a small smile along the way) goes a long way.

CONCLUSION

If this book helped you feel more informed, more prepared, or more confident about your financial decisions, then it's done exactly what it was meant to do.

Please do not ever hesitate to reach out to me at:

tbyrnes@lebenthal.com
@tracybyrnes on LinkedIn

My best,
Tracy

APPENDIX A

Recordkeeping That Actually Saves You Money

If you want to pay less in taxes—legally and confidently—recordkeeping is where it starts.

Under the One Big Beautiful Bill Act (OBBBA), the IRS is moving aggressively toward real-time digital matching. That means good records aren't just helpful anymore—they're your first line of defense and the reason you're able to claim deductions in the first place.

The days of the "paper shoebox" are officially over. In a digital-first tax system, disorganization isn't just inconvenient—it's a liability.

The good news? This doesn't have to be complicated. You don't need perfection. You just need a system that works consistently.

Start with the One Number That Drives Everything: AGI

You've seen me reference AGI (adjusted gross income) throughout this book because it sits at the center of your entire tax life.

Where to find it: As mentioned before, for the 2026 filing season, your AGI appears on Line 11 of Form 1040.

Here is why it matters.

Your AGI determines eligibility for:

- The expanded SALT deduction
- Senior bonus deductions
- Child-related credits and phaseouts
- Medical expense deductions
- Many OBBBA-era benefits that quietly disappear above certain income levels

And get that number off last year's return so you have it handy.

The Records You Need to Keep (So You Can Defend Every Deduction)

Income Records

- W-2s and 1099s, including Form 1099-DA for digital asset transactions
- Pay stubs, especially your final year-to-date stub
- Tipped income logs (daily tracking is now required)
- Overtime pay documentation
- Bank and brokerage statements
- Rental income records
- Retirement distributions
- Asset sales
- Awards, prizes, gambling income, and canceled debt
- Inherited assets

Expense and Deduction Records

- Mileage logs (GPS-based preferred)
- Medical expenses and qualified LTC premiums
- Charitable contribution receipts
- Vehicle loan statements
- Property tax and registration documents
- Estimated tax payment records
- Home improvement receipts
- Business-related expenses

Your Digital Audit Trail: Tools That Work in 2026

Some Suggested Apps

Money tracking:

- Monarch Money
- QuickBooks Self-Employed

Receipt capture:

- Shoeboxed
- Expensify

Mileage tracking:

- MileIQ

How Long to Keep Records

- **Tax returns.** Keep forever (seriously)
- **Supporting documents.** Keep at least 7 years
- **Property records.** Keep 7 years after sale

Final Thought

Good recordkeeping isn't about fear. It's about control. When your records are clean, you claim deductions confidently, respond calmly to IRS questions, and stop leaving money on the table.

APPENDIX B

DIY Versus Hiring a Tax Pro

Knowing When to Call in Help

One of the most common questions I hear is: "Should I be doing my own taxes—or paying someone else to do them?"

The honest answer is: it depends.

Doing your own taxes isn't inherently risky. For many people, it's perfectly reasonable. The problem arises when complexity quietly creeps in and no one tells you that you've crossed the line where DIY stops saving money and starts costing it.

This appendix is here to help you recognize that line—calmly, confidently, and without judgment.

When DIY Usually Works Just Fine

Preparing your own tax return can make sense if most of the following are true:

- Your income comes primarily from a W-2
- You don't own a business or rental property

- You don't have significant investment activity
- You didn't move states, sell property, or experience a major life change
- Your deductions are straightforward
- Your return looks mostly the same from year to year

In these situations, reputable tax software can be a perfectly reasonable tool—especially when paired with strong recordkeeping.

Where DIY Starts to Break Down

Complexity doesn't usually arrive all at once. It sneaks in.

You may want to consider professional help if any of the following apply:

- You're self-employed, freelancing, or running a side business
- You receive multiple 1099s
- You own rental property or short-term rentals
- You sold a home, business, or large investment
- You exercised stock options or received equity compensation
- You have digital asset transactions
- You moved states or have multi-state income
- Your income jumped significantly from one year to the next
- You're nearing retirement or drawing income from multiple sources
- You're trying to take advantage of new OBBBA-era provisions

At this stage, tax preparation becomes less about forms—and more about strategy.

The Cost Question

Many people hesitate to hire a tax professional because of cost.

But think about it: the right professional doesn't just prepare your return—she helps you avoid expensive mistakes, missed deductions, and planning blind spots that can cost far more than their fee.

The question isn't "Can I do this myself?" It's "What is the risk of getting this wrong?"

What a Good Tax Pro Actually Does

A good tax professional should:

- Ask better questions than software ever could
- Flag issues before they become problems
- Help you plan ahead —not just look backward
- Explain decisions in plain English
- Coordinate with your other advisors (like me!) when appropriate

If all you're getting is data entry, you're not getting full value.

How to Get the Most Value from a Tax Professional

Hiring a tax pro doesn't mean handing everything over blindly. You'll get better results if you:

- Keep clean records
- Come prepared with questions

- Share upcoming life changes before they happen
- Understand that planning happens during the year—not just in April

The best outcomes come from collaboration, not delegation.

Red Flags to Watch For

Consider a second opinion if your tax preparer:

- Can't explain your return clearly
- Never discusses planning opportunities
- Avoids questions or dismisses your concerns
- Treats every client exactly the same

One Final Thought

Doing your own taxes doesn't make you careless. Hiring a professional doesn't make you incapable.

Smart people choose tools—and partners—that fit their lives.

The goal isn't to prove you can do it yourself. The goal is to make informed decisions, protect your money, and move forward with confidence.

And sometimes, the smartest move is knowing when to ask for help.

APPENDIX C

I Need a Tax Pro

How Do I Find the Right One for Me?

Who's Who in the Tax World

Enrolled Agents (EAs)

Tax specialists licensed by the IRS. Excellent for individual and business taxes, audits, and tax debt.

CPAs

Broad financial professionals. Great for complex returns, businesses, and long-term planning.

Tax Attorneys

Best for legal disputes, estates, business structures, or criminal tax matters—not routine returns.

Big note: Most people do not need an attorney. Many people benefit from an EA or CPA sooner than they think.

Red Flags—Run, Don't Walk

Be cautious if a preparer:

- Promises a "huge refund" without explaining why
- Won't clearly explain your return
- Refuses to sign the return as the preparer
- Pushes refund loans or advance products
- Treats every client exactly the same

If it feels sketchy, it probably is.

How to Get the Most Value from a Tax Pro

You'll get better results if you:

- Keep clean records (Appendix A matters)
- Ask planning questions before April
- Share life changes before they happen
- Schedule a planning conversation mid-year
- Treat the relationship as ongoing, not transactional

One hour of planning can save years of cleanup.

One Last Thing

You are always responsible for what's on your tax return—even if someone else prepares it.

So read it.

Ask questions.

And don't sign anything you don't understand.

Smart tax decisions aren't about fear. They're about awareness, timing, and knowing when to ask for help.

APPENDIX D

Think About State Taxes Before You Move

Every year, I see headlines declaring the "best" and "worst" states for taxes, retirement, or quality of life. And every year, I have clients ask the same question:

"Should I move?"

Sometimes the answer is yes.

Often, it's not.

And occasionally, it's absolutely not—even if the rankings say otherwise.

This appendix is here to help you think through state taxes intelligently, without chasing headlines or making expensive assumptions.

Here's a Reality Check: There Is No Such Thing as a "Tax-Free" State

States that advertise "no income tax" still have to fund schools, roads, emergency services, and healthcare. They just collect revenue differently.

That usually means:

- Higher sales taxes
- Higher property taxes
- Higher insurance costs
- Higher fees and assessments

In other words, the tax bill doesn't disappear—it just changes form.

Before you get excited about a zero-income-tax headline, ask: What am I paying instead?

Income Tax Is Only One Piece of the Puzzle

State income tax matters most when:

- You're still working
- You have high earned income
- You receive pass-through business income

But for retirees, investors, and business owners, other factors often matter more:

- How the state taxes retirement income
- Capital gains treatment
- Estate or inheritance taxes
- Property taxes over time
- Healthcare access and costs

A state can look "tax-friendly" on paper and still be expensive in real life.

When Moving for Tax Reasons Can Make Sense

A move may be worth exploring if:

- You're retiring and no longer tied to a job location
- You're exiting a business or planning a liquidity event
- You're transitioning to remote work permanently
- You're planning long-term residency (not part-time)

Timing matters. Moving before a major income event can be very different from moving after.

Residency Rules Matter More Than You Think

This is where people get into trouble.

States care deeply about residency—especially high-tax states. Simply owning a home elsewhere or spending "most" of the year in a new state may not be enough.

Residency audits look at:

- Where you spend time
- Where you vote
- Where your doctors are
- Where your financial accounts are registered
- Where your "center of life" exists

Getting this wrong can mean paying taxes in two states.

This is one of the biggest reasons to consult a professional before making a move.

Rankings Are Tolls—Not Instructions

Indexes from groups like the Tax Foundation or Bankrate can be helpful starting points.

But they don't know:

- Your income mix
- Your family situation
- Your health needs
- Your lifestyle priorities
- Your long-term plans

A "top-ranked" state for someone else may be a poor fit for you.

Before You Move, Ask Yourself

- Am I optimizing for taxes—or for quality of life?
- Is this a permanent move or a temporary one?
- How will this affect my healthcare, family, and support systems?
- Am I moving before or after a major financial event?
- Have I confirmed residency rules with a professional?

If you can't answer these clearly, pause before packing boxes.

One Final Thought

Taxes matter—but they're only part of the equation.

The goal isn't to live in the lowest-tax state possible.

The goal is to live well, plan intelligently, and avoid costly mistakes.

When state taxes become part of a broader financial plan—not the sole driver—you're far more likely to end up in the right place, for the right reasons.

Acknowledgments

This book happened because a few very important people showed up when it mattered.

Keith Pfeffer—thank you for giving me the opportunity to write another book and for believing in this one from the start.

Patty Wallenburg—you led this project with clarity, calm, and momentum. Thank you for keeping it moving, keeping it together, and keeping me sane.

Judy and Alison—thank you for your careful eye, thoughtful guidance, and expertise to help bring this book across the finish line.

Cheryl, Kim, and Illana—thank you for everything: the support, the honesty, the giggles, and the constant reminder that I'm never doing this life alone.

To my parents—your love, encouragement, and steady support have carried me further than you know.

Frank—thank you for letting me go be me and for always making me laugh when I need it most. I love you.

And to my kids—thank you for pushing me to be better every day. You are the reason I keep building, learning, and showing up. I love you most.

Index

Above-the-line deductions, 10–11, 41–42, 74, 109, 131
Adoption credit, 53
Advertising wraps, 141
Age-based tax relief for medical expenses, 27
AGI (Adjusted gross income):
  and above-the-line deductions, 42
  and charitable giving, 5, 87
  deduction limits for, 91
  and Identity Protection PINs, 166
  importance of, 185–186
  and long-term care, 29–30
  and medical expense threshold, 21, 28
  medical expenses effect on, 54, 110, 143
  myths about, 152
  and PMI deductions, 63
  qualified charitable distributions effect on, 26
  and Social Security, 19–20
Aging-in-place financial support credit, 26–28
Airbnb hosting, 73, 81
Allocated tips, 45
Alternative fuel refueling property credit, 65–66

Amended returns, 162–163, 175
Amended U.S. Individual Income Tax Return (Form 1040-X), 162–163
American Opportunity Tax Credit (AOTC), 53–54
Annual contributions maximization, 32
Annual gift tax exclusion, 57–58
Anti-abuse rules, 17
Application for Automatic Extension of Time to File (Form 4868), 158–159
Appreciated asset donations, 92, 94, 114
Appreciated stock donations, 90–91, 93, 114
Audits, 171–180
  and business meals, 100
  and cash donations, 87–88
  of cash-heavy businesses, 174
  digitization for, 12, 187
  and DMSH, 109
  from EITC claims, 175
  fixes for, 180
  from home office deductions, 108, 174
  myths about, 147, 155–156
  from overvaluation, 88
  receipts for, 177

Audits (*continued*):
  residency, 199
  of S Corporations, 106
  strategies for, 176–180
  tax pros for, 193
  and tax records, 169
  tip reporting as trigger for, 44, 140
  types of, 177
Auto deductions, 135–142
  advertising wrap, 141
  buying vs. leasing, 144
  charitable mileage, 142
  depreciation, 143–144
  gross vehicle weigh rating for, 139
  medical mileage, 143
  mileage, 101–102, 108, 173, 178, 187
  parking and tolls, 141–142
  property tax, 144

Backdoor Roth IRAs, 122
Bonus depreciation, 79, 107, 144
  (*See also* Depreciation)
Bunching strategies, 86, 92
Business accounts, 81
Business expenses:
  DMSH Rule for, 108
  home office, 101, 108, 139–140, 151, 174
  logging, 136
  meals, 76, 100–101, 103, 150, 173
  mileage, 101–102, 108
  myths about, 147–155
  records for, 187
  tracking, 180
  for travel, 103
  vehicles, 135–142, 173
  See also Travel expenses
Business owners, 8–9, 73, 99, 104, 108, 109, 131, 139, 198

Business taxes, 102, 193
Business travel (*see* Travel expenses)

C Corporations (C Corps), 105–106
Capital gains, 112–115
  and appreciate stock donations, 91
  avoiding, 91, 93, 114
  and charitable remainder trusts, 94
  crypto as, 117
  deferring, 94
  and donor-advised funds, 93
  gifting of, 58
  home sales as, 66–67
  investment property sales as, 68
  long-term, 112–113, 117
  net investment income as, 125, 128
  short-term, 112
  state treatment of, 198
  tax bracket management for, 114
  tax-free growth of, 133
  tax-loss harvesting for, 113–114
Caregiving, 26–28, 143
Carry forward excess gifts, 91
Cash App, 46
Cash donations, 87–89
Cash method of accounting, 106–107
Cash-heavy businesses, 174
Catch-up contributions, 11–12, 22, 121
CDCTC (Child and Dependent Care Tax Credit), 27
CGA (Charitable gift annuity), 26
Charitable deductions, 85–97
  AGI deduction limits for, 91
  for appreciated assets, 114
  appreciated stock as, 90
  bunching strategies for, 86, 91
  cash donations for, 87–89

INDEX

clothing and household goods as, 88
documentation for, 86
donor-advised funds (DAFs) for, 92–94
for IRA funds, 124
IRS documentation rules for, 12
itemizing, 3, 5, 26, 85–86
mileage for, 55, 142
net gift, 90
OBBBA changes in, 96–97
parking and tolls, 142
qualified charitable distributions for, 91
vehicle donations as, 89–90
See also Qualified charitable distribution (QCD)
Charitable gift annuity (CGA), 26
Charitable remainder annuity trusts (CRATs), 95–96
Charitable remainder trusts (CRTs), 26, 94–96
Charitable remainder unitrusts (CRUTs), 95–96
Charities, 86–90
Child and Dependent Care (CDC) Credit, 52, 55, 155
Child and Dependent Care Tax Credit (CDCTC), 27
Child employment, 57–58
Child tax credit (CTC), 5, 52, 155
Client entertainment deduction, 150
Closing costs deduction, 65
Closing statements (HUD-1), 77
Clothing deduction, 149
Compensation reclassification, 17
CP2000 notices, 173
CPAs, 136, 178, 182, 193
CRATs (Charitable remainder annuity trusts), 95–96
Credit card tax payments, 161

CRTs (Charitable remainder trusts), 26, 94–96
CRUTs (Charitable remainder unitrusts), 95–96
Cryptocurrency, 116–117
de minimis exemption for, 117
holding of, 112, 117
index-based investments vs., 33
mining and staking, 116
myths about, 153
in Trump accounts, 35
wash sale loophole for, 116
CTC (Child tax credit), 5, 52, 155

DAFs (Donor-advised funds), 92–94
De minimis exemption, 117
De Minimis Safe Harbor (DMSH) rule, 108–109
Dell Foundation, 34
Depreciation:
on boats, 150
client entertainment costs, 150
DMSH Rule vs., 108
of equipment, 107
of home offices, 108–109
on leased cars, 144
luxury car, 138–139
mileage deduction as, 143–144
as phantom deduction, 74–75
of qualified improvements, 79–80
on rental properties, 68, 74–75
Section 179 vs., 107
and standard mileage rate (SMR), 138, 143–144
of used property, 107
Diaz, Cameron, 71
Digital assets (*see* Cryptocurrency)
Direct Pay, 160
Divorce deduction, 150
DMSH (De Minimis Safe Harbor) rule, 108–109

Donor-advised funds (DAFs), 92–94

Earned income:
   and CDC credit, 52
   deduction limits on, 110
   and innocent spouse relief, 167
   and Roth IRAs, 57, 122
   from self-employment, 109–110
   state taxes on, 198
Earned income tax credit (EITC), 52, 155, 162, 174–175
Electronic Federal Tax Payment System (EFTPS), 160
Electronic filing, 158, 162
Employee safety costs, 103
Employer match, 33
Employer plans, 110
Employer reimbursements, 144–145
Enrolled agents (EAs), 178, 193
Equitable relief, 168
Escrow taxes, 77
Estate and gift tax, 6, 124
ETFs, 32, 33, 35, 115
EV charger installation costs deduction, 65
Expanded saver's credit, 23–24
Expensify, 187
Extensions, 157–169
   credit card payments for, 161–162
   deadline for, 158–159
   e-filing for, 158, 160
   form 1040 x (Amended U.S.Individual Income Tax Return) for, 162–163
   form 4868 for, 158–159
   interest payments on, 163–164
   payment plans for, 160–161
   and payments, 159–160
   and penalty abatements, 163
   short-term payment, 161
   for state returns, 163

Fair Labor Standards Act (FLSA) rules, 13–17
Fair market value (FMV), 134
Family legacies, 2, 26, 51, 95
Ferris Bueller's Day Off (film), 135, 138, 145
FICA taxes:
   on overtime, 15
   for self-employment, 45
   on Social Security, 11
   on tips, 39–44
   uncollected, 44
Filing deadlines, 177
   for 1099s, 77
   and audits, 177
   extensions to, 157–157
   importance of, 159
   for rollovers, 130
   for Roth IRAs, 171
   for state returns, 163
Financial advisors, 5, 9, 132, 182
First-Time Penalty Abatement (FTA), 163
501(c)(3) organizations, 86
$500 Rule, 172
529 plans, 34, 36–37, 56–57
Flexible spending accounts (FSAs), 55
Form 1040-X (Amended U.S. Individual Income Tax Return), 162–163
Form 1098-C, 89
Form 1099, 149, 168, 172–174, 176
Form 1099-DA, 186
Form 1099-K, 46, 77–78
Form 1099-MISC, 77–78
Form 4868 (Application for Automatic Extension of Time to File), 158
Form 8606, 121
Form 8857, 74, 168–169

INDEX

Form W-2:
  allocated tips on, 45–46
  for children, 179
  mismatched, 176
  overtime on, 15
  record-keeping for, 186
  requirements for, 9
  service charges on, 48
  Two-year reporting transition for, 16
  uncollected FICA on, 44
Form W-9, 77
401(k) accounts:
  contribution limits to, 11, 22
  loan repayment on, 123
  net investment income tax application to, 126
  required minimum distributions from, 133
  Roth, 11, 122
  as smart contribution, 126
  withdrawals from, 20, 128
  See also IRAs (traditional); Roth IRAs
14-day rental loophole, 72
FTA (First-Time Penalty Abatement), 163

Goodfellas (film), 138, 171, 176, 177, 180
Grandfathered loans, 62
Gross Vehicle Weight Rating (GVWR), 139
Grumpy Old Men (film), 18, 31

Hanks, Tom, 61, 69
Head of Household (HOH) filing status, 19, 52, 58, 127
Health deduction, 151
Health savings accounts (HSAs), 14–15, 55, 126, 131–134
High-deductible health plans (HDHPs), 55, 132

Hill, Henry, 171, 179, 180
Hobby businesses, 80, 154, 175–176
The Holiday (film), 71, 83
Home basis, 65, 67–68
Home Equity Line of Credit (HELOC), 63
Home offices, 101, 108, 139–140, 151, 174
Home sale exclusion, 66–68
HR and payroll teams (training for), 17
HSAs (Health savings accounts), 14–15, 55, 126, 131–134
HUD-1 (Closing statements), 77

Identity protection PINs (IP PINs), 165–166
Identity theft, 165
Index-based investments, 33–34
Individual Taxpayer Identification Number (ITIN), 165
Injured spouses, 166–168
Innocent spouses, 167–168
Interest:
  on borrowed money, 81
  on car loans, 10, 138
  and charitable giving, 94, 96
  on credit cards, 161
  daily accrual of, 82
  on grandfathered loans, 62
  HELOC, 63
  as home office deduction, 108
  and innocent spouse relief, 168
  itemizing, 85–86
  and kiddie tax rule, 58
  mortgage, 3, 62, 64, 76
  on municipal bonds, 127, 128
  as net investment income, 125, 128
  penalties on, 154–155, 160–161, 163
  prepaid, 65

Interest (*continued*):
  to private lenders, 80
  student loan, 54, 56
  tax-free growth of, 133
  on time-shares, 79
  from uncollected FICA, 44
  on unpaid loans, 82
Interest paid before closing deduction, 65
Investment fee deduction, 129
IRAs (traditional):
  charitable deductions for, 25–26, 87, 91, 124
  contributing to, 32, 119–121
  conversion to Roth, 123
  early withdrawal penalties for, 123
  fees for, 129
  401(k) rollovers to, 123
  HSAs vs., 133
  as net investment income, 126, 128
  nondeductible contributions to, 121–122
  out-of-pocket fees for, 129
  and saver's match, 23–24
  as smart contribution, 126
  Trump accounts as, 33, 35, 56
  withdrawal taxes on, 20, 28
  (*See also* 401(k) accounts; Roth IRAs)
IRS digital documentation rules, 12
IRS online accounts, 164–166, 168
Itemized deductions, 3, 5, 19, 42, 76, 85–86, 93, 96

Kid credits, 52–53
Kiddie tax rule, 58

Law, Jude, 71, 83
Lifetime Learning Credit (LLC), 8, 53–54

LLCs, 9, 104, 159
Local hotel/lodging tax laws, 81
Long, Shelley, 61
Long term investing, 112
Long-term care (LTC) deductions, 28–31, 109
Long-term rental properties, 73–74
Long-term savings, 119
Luxury car depreciation limits, 138
Lyft, 140

MAGI (Modified adjusted gross income):
  affects on deductions, 14–15, 126
  limits for QBI deductions, 105
  lowering, 126
  municipal bond sales as, 127
  and Roth IRA eligibility, 120–121
  Roth withdrawals as, 126
  and SALT deduction, 4
  for seniors, 23
  threshold of, 125–129
Married filing jointly status:
  CDC credit for, 52
  deduction limit for, 14–15
  and injured spouse relief, 166
  and NIIT, 127
  and QBI deduction, 105
  and Roth IRA contributions, 121
  and saver's credit, 24
  senior deduction limit for, 19
  and Social Security, 20
  and tip deductions, 41
Medical expense threshold, 20–21
Medical expenses:
  age-based tax relief for, 27
  AGI eligibility for, 186
  for dependents, 54
  as earned income deduction, 110
  health savings accounts (HSAs) for, 55, 133–134

INDEX

and long-term care, 28–31
medically necessary home improvements as, 68
mileage, 143
myths about, 152
record-keeping for, 187
and standard deduction, 2–3
Medical mileage, 143
Medically necessary home improvements deduction, 68
Medicare, 10, 15, 26, 40–43, 57, 73, 103, 106, 132
Mileage:
   and advertising wraps, 141
   as business expense, 101–102, 108
   charitable, 55, 142
   as home office expense, 108, 139–140
   IRS rules for, 12
   logging, 173, 178, 187
   medical, 143
   as ordinary and necessary expense, 187–188
   and parking, 142
   reimbursement for, 144
   from rideshares, 140
   standard rate (SMR), 101, 108, 136–138, 143–144
   tracking apps for, 102, 187–188
MileIQ, 187
Mining and staking tax deferments, 116
Monarch Money, 187
The Money Pit (film), 61, 69
Mortgage interest deduction, 3, 62, 76, 79, 80, 85, 108
Mortgage points on purchase deduction, 64
Moving expenses, 143
Multiple Jobs, 48–49
Municipal bonds, 127

Net gift donations, 90
Net Investment Income Tax (NIIT), 124–129
Newborn Savings Accounts, 56
   (*See also* Trump Accounts)
Nondeductible IRA contributions, 121–122
Notice of deficiency, 177

Office-in-home deduction (*see* Home offices)
Online Payments, 160
Ordinary and necessary expense deduction, 72, 102
Overtime:
   as above-the-line deduction, 10
   FICA taxes on, 15
   FLSA premium deduction for, 14, 17
   HR training for, 17
   qualified, 15, 16
   records for, 186
   state laws for, 17–18
   tips for employers, 15–16
   tracking, 13–14
Overtime premium, 15–16

Parking and tolls, 102, 141–142
Partnerships, 9, 57, 104, 110, 158
Passive activity loss, 73, 82
Pay Stubs, 15
Payment Plans, 160
PayPal Goods & Services, 78
Penalties, 163
Personal home to rental deduction, 76
Personal tax rates, 4
Pet deduction, 148
Phantom deduction, 71–72, 74–75
   (*see also* Depreciation)
Phaseout range, 121
Private fund management fees, 130

Private lender interest deduction, 80
Private mortgage insurance (PMI) deduction, 63
Profit motive, 80
Property taxes paid deduction, 63
   for businesses, 102
   for buyers and sellers, 77
   at closing, 64
   personal, 144
   for rentals, 74, 76
   SALT deduction vs., 4, 62
   standard deduction vs., 3
Protecting Americans from Tax Hikes (PATH) Act, 162

Qualified Business Income Deduction (QBID), 8–9, 104–105
Qualified Charitable Distribution (QCD), 25–26, 87, 91–92, 124 (*See also* Charitable deductions)
Qualified improvements depreciation, 79
Qualified Small Business Stock (QSBS) rules, 8–10
Qualifying widow(er) status, 58–59
QuickBooks self-employed, 187

Receipts:
   actual amounts from, 172
   apps for, 187
   for audits, 177–178
   for business meals, 100, 103, 173
   in cash accounting, 106
   from cash donations, 87
   for charitable deductions, 12, 92–93, 187
   for home basis, 67–68
   from medical bills, 133
   for mileage, 137–138, 142, 145
   need for, 154
   from parking and tolls, 102
   from refinancing, 81
   tracking, 73
Record-keeping, 185–188
Refinance deductions, 64–65, 81
Refinance funds, 81
Refund and payment tracking, 162
Rental properties, 71–83
   Airbnbs as, 73
   business accounts for, 81
   business use taxes on, 74
   conversion of, 68
   cost of attracting guests for, 75
   credit card payments for, 78
   deductions for, 79–82
   depreciation on, 74
   and escrow taxes, 77
   forms for service providers, 77
   14-day loophole for, 72
   hacks for, 71
   hotel taxes on, 81
   long-term, 73–74
   ordinary and necessary expense deduction for, 72
   passive activity loss limitations for, 82
   personal home deduction for, 76
   private lender interest for, 80
   profit motive for, 80
   qualified improvement depreciation for, 79–80
   reporting for, 73–78
   time-share interest deduction for, 79
   travel expense deduction for, 75–76
   unpaid interest on, 82
Required minimum distributions (RMDs), 21–22, 26, 122, 124

INDEX

Residency audits, 199
Retirement plans (*see* 401(k) accounts; IRAs (traditional); Roth IRAs)
Retirement Savings Contributions Credit, 23–24
Rideshare drivers, 12, 46, 140
Rollover deadlines, 130
Roth 401(k) accounts, 11, 122
  (*See also* 401(k) accounts)
Roth IRAs:
  backdoor, 122
  for children, 57–58, 122
  contributing to, 121
  conversion of, 123, 130
  mandatory catch-up rule for, 11–12
  maximum contribution to, 121
  required minimum distributions for, 22
  strategic use of, 126
  tax-free nature of, 119–120
  Trump account conversions to, 33
  See also 401(k) accounts; IRAs (traditional)

S Corporations (S corps), 9, 104, 106, 110, 158
SALT (State and Local Taxes) deduction, 3, 4, 62–64, 74, 102, 186
Saver's credit, 23–24
Saver's match, 23, 25
Schedule A, 29, 85–86, 110, 143
Schedule C, 9, 73, 110, 136, 141
Schedule E, 73
Section 179 expensing, 107–109, 139
Section 280A(g), 72
Section 446 deductions, 82
Section 6041, 77
Section 6050H, 80
SECURE (Setting Every Community Up for Retirement Enhancement) Act, 21, 57
Self-employment, 46, 73–74, 102
  business meal deductions for, 100
  business tax deductions for, 102
  DIY filing for, 190
  health insurance deduction for, 109–110, 140
  income from, 126, 128
  mileage deductions for, 101–102
  parking and tolls deductions for, 102
  QBI deductions for, 104–105
  Social Security credits for, 104
  taxes on, 42, 45, 46, 103, 104, 106, 140
  tip deductions for, 56
  for tipped employees, 41
  travel expenses for, 103
Senior deduction, 18–19
Separation of liability, 168
Service charges, 47–48
Setting Every Community Up for Retirement Enhancement (SECURE) Act, 21, 57
Settlement sheets, 64, 77
Shoeboxed, 187
Shopify payments, 78
Short-term payment extensions, 161
Side cash, 153
Single filing status:
  CDC credit for, 52
  deduction limit for, 14–15
  head of household vs., 58
  home sales exclusion for, 66–67
  and QBI deduction, 105
  and Roth IRA eligibility, 120–121
  senior deduction limits for, 18–19

Single filing status (*continued*):
  and Social Security, 20
  and tip deductions, 41
Small-business owners, 8–10, 12, 73, 99, 104, 106, 108, 109 (*See also* Business owners)
Smart contributions, 126
SMR (Standard mileage rate), 101, 108, 136–138, 143–144
Social Security benefits, 19
  and above the line deductions, 43
  and aging in place, 28
  for children, 57
  credits for, 104
  FICA taxes on, 41, 43
  Net Investment Income Tax (NIIT) on, 125, 128
  under OBBBA, 19–20
  and overtime, 15
  payroll taxes on, 106
  and qualified charitable distributions, 26
  and Roth catch-up rule, 11
  self-employment tax on, 73, 103
  and tax filing, 155, 158, 165
  tip reporting for, 40, 45
Social Security numbers (SSNs), 165
Social Security tax trap, 19–20
Sole proprietorships, 9, 57, 104, 110
Square, 78
Standard deduction, 2–3
  and bunching strategy, 86
  and child employment, 57
  and donor-advised funds (DAFs), 92–94
  for head of household, 58
  itemizing vs., 86
  for qualifying widow(er) status, 59

  raising of, 61
  and self-employed health insurance deduction, 109
  for seniors, 18–19
  for tipped workers, 41–43
Standard mileage rate (SMR), 101, 108, 136–138, 143–144
State and local taxes (SALT) deduction (*see* SALT (state and local taxes) deduction)
State taxes, 91, 163, 197–201
Stealth NIIT Tax, 111
Stripe, 78
Student loans, 54, 56–57, 167

Tax attorneys, 178, 193
Tax brackets, 12, 42, 51, 58, 105, 112, 114, 130
Tax credits:
  adoption, 53
  and AGI, 42
  caregiving, 27
  child, 5, 52–53, 155
  earned income, 52, 162, 174
  for education, 53–54
  for seniors, 23
  tax deductions vs, 24, 51
Tax Cuts and Jobs Act (TCJA), 2*t*, 4, 6–8, 61, 62, 129, 143
Tax deferral, 21–22, 25–26, 33, 94, 105, 116, 121
Tax deferred growth, 32
Tax exclusions:
  annual gift tax, 57–58
  estate and gift tax, 124
  home sale, 66–68
  OBBBA increases to, 9–10
  rental property, 68–69
Tax ID number, 77
Tax prep cost deduction, 129
Tax preparers, 77, 82, 141, 182, 192
Tax professionals, 178

INDEX

Tax records, 169
Tax shelters, 8, 61–69
Taxable withdrawals after age 18, 33
Tax-deferred growth, 32, 121
Tax-loss harvesting, 113–114
TCJA (Tax Cuts and Jobs Act), 2t, 4, 6–8, 61, 62, 129, 143
1099-K, 153
Thrift Savings Plans (TSPs), 34
Time-share interest deduction, 79
Tips, 39–48, 140
   $25,000 deduction for, 41, 46
   allocated, 45
   daily records for, 40
   electronic, 46–47
   federal vs. state deductions for, 48
   and FICA, 43
   Monitoring of, 47
   pooled, 43
   reporting, 40, 45
   and service charges, 47–48
   uncollected FICA, 44
   unreported, 45
Transient occupancy taxes, 81
Travel expenses:
   and adoption credit, 53
   business meals, 100–101
   deducting, 103
   deduction for rental properties, 75–76
   and home-office deductions, 108, 139–140
   parking and tolls, 102, 141
   See also Business expenses
Treasury Department, 33, 35
Triple tax advantage, 55, 131–134
Trump Accounts, 32–37, 56
TSPs (Thrift Savings Plans), 34
Two-Year W-2 reporting transition, 16

Uber, 140
Uncollected FICA taxes, 44
Uniform Transfers to Minors Act (UTMA), 34
Unpaid interest from loans, 82
Unreported income, 45, 153, 172–173, 178
Un-retiring, 22, 23–24
Used property depreciation, 107

Vacation deduction, 149
Vacation Rental Losses, 154
Vehicle business use, 135–142, 173
Vehicle donations, 89–90
Venmo, 44, 46, 87, 140, 153, 157

Wash sale rule, 113, 115
Wedding deduction, 148

Zelle, 46

About the Author

TRACY BYRNES is Vice President of Women & Investing at Lebenthal Global Advisors, and has spent decades working at the intersection of money, markets, and tax policy—and translating all three into clear language anyone can understand. A financial journalist for over thirty years, covering tax, accounting, and personal finance issues, she is a contributor to NEWSMAX, and has been an on-air reporter for the FOX Business Network, and has written weekly finance columns for the *New York Post* and TheStreet.com. Byrnes spent five years as a senior accountant with Ernst & Young LLP, has an MBA in accounting from Rutgers University, and is the author of *Break Down Your Money: How to Get Beyond the Noise to Profit in the Markets*.

Learn more about tax strategies and financial freedom at TracyByrnesWealth.com.